MAISON BOUTURE

Seeds & cuttings

Olivia Brun

Tiphaine Germain-Lacour

GINGKO PRESS

Gardening provides time for yourself—to reflect, think, and reconnect—with the nature that awakens before us! Having an outdoor garden is not necessary to enjoy these moments of delight; it is quite possible to create an indoor garden to get closer to nature and breathe healthy air. This is why we created Maison Bouture—to provide access to nature, which offers a soothing escape for everyone.

Maison Bouture sets up "plant getaways" in the heart of cities in the form of Ephemeral Gardens: green settings where you can rest and recharge. These getaways are also meeting places for enthusiasts and the curious, where one can get valuable advice and obtain cuttings of plants; a relaxing pause in our daily lives, which are sometimes punctuated by nonessential things!

This book is the fruit of our experiments and observations, which allows us to share and provide access to a garden that is easy to savor and contemplate.

Tiphaine

Olivia

Contents

Introduction

Gardening, like reading a book, watching a movie, walking on a beach or in the mountains, is an escape. Taking the time to take care of your plants, to feed them, to prune them, to repot them, to take cuttings, to watch them grow and become more beautiful, can be a source of tranquility. It is so good to marvel at a seed, a pit, a stem or even just a leaf that will grow into a plant. And when a new leaf appears or a new root gently unfolds before your eyes, it is an exhilarating sight!

Cutting and multiplying your plants is a very simple pleasure that will make you discover the wonders at your fingertips, even if you think yours are not green!

Before beginning, however simple it may be, it is useful to have a few notes to maximize the success of your cuttings and the germination of your pits and seeds.

What is germination?

Germination marks the beginning of the growth of a plant from a pit or a seed. Coming out of their dormancy in contact with humidity and heat, seeds will open to reveal a small rootlet, thus marking the birth of a new plant!

The conditions for success

For some species, the awakening of the pit or the seed will be made possible by placing it in the refrigerator in order to simulate a winter temperature. When your seedling first stirs, prompted by a humid heat, the spring-like conditions will allow it to take root. Some pits and stones (like the pit of the mango) must be sheltered from the light, while others, on the contrary, benefit from a lot of light to promote germination (this is the case with citrus pips).

Germination materials

There are purpose-built germination trays for seeds, but you will see that by rummaging through your cupboards, you can probably find everything you need!

- **A SMALL CONTAINER**, such as a glass or the lid of a jam jar, may be used for seed germination.
- **PAPER TOWELS OR COTTON** to enclose the seeds and keep them moist.

- **A GLASS VASE** to germinate in water. Its transparency offers full light to the roots that develop there and also allows them to be seen while they are growing.
- **A FUNNEL** (or the neck of a plastic bottle) to place at the top of a vase. It holds the seeds once germinated, which are thus kept moist.
- **SMALL POTS** for seedlings or for sowing seeds.
- **POTS WITH HOLES** in the bottom will allow you to put your cuttings in soil after germination. Glazed or plastic pots with drainage will allow the roots to breathe and maintain humidity.
- **SOIL** of different types depending on the plants and their stage of growth, such as seedling soil, citrus soil, cactus, or a general potting mix.

What are cuttings?

Cutting consists of giving birth to a new shoot by taking a fragment of a so-called "mother" plant. By following the appropriate technique, you will create a plant that will have the same DNA as the mother: the same color, same foliage, same size, and etc. This is why it is important to take cuttings from healthy plants that show no signs of disease.
This method does not involve the germination of a seed. When you cut a stem or a leaf, the lesion will heal to form a callus, i.e., a small dry crust. This is where the future roots will regenerate and allow the development of a new plant. However, we will see that for some species it is not necessary to wait for a callus to form. Indeed, fine-leaved plants experience great stress when they are detached from their mother. They wither and soften, so they must be quickly put in soil or in water. On the other hand, succulents and cacti, which store water in their leaves, will tend to rot if placed directly in moist potting soil or in water. For these species, it is necessary to wait for the formation of the callus, which will prevent any infection.
It is incredible to see that a simple plant fragment, when well chosen, has the ability to produce new roots to become, in a just few weeks or a few months, a plant in its own right.

Why take cuttings?

Cuttings are above all a pleasure! That of reproducing a plant to infinity, for oneself or to offer to others. It's sharing, joy, discoveries, an invitation to contemplation!

Cuttings also make it possible to replenish a somewhat dull plant, which has lost its aesthetic appearance. Just plant your cutting at the foot of the mother plant to give it a boost! Conversely, it can refresh a plant that is becoming too bushy: instead of pruning the stems and throwing them away, take cuttings! They will be nice gifts to give to your friends.

The conditions for success

In order to increase your chances of success, it is essential to choose your cuttings carefully. The mother plant from which you take them should be healthy and show no signs of disease or pests. Depending on the plants, only certain parts are suitable for cuttings. But everything in its time; we will explain all this to you in the pages to come!

A suitable material

- **PRUNERS** are preferable to scissors which tend to crush the cutting. Your equipment must be clean and disinfected with alcohol. Indeed, the cuttings are fragile and can quickly be exposed to rot, disease, or attacks by pests. For euphorbias and cacti, you will need a sharp knife to make clean cuts.
- **THE MISTER** is an indispensable tool. It is very useful for leaf cuttings and gently moistens the soil without wetting the foliage. It will also be a must for the maintenance of plants that need constant humidity.
- **A PIECE OF CHARCOAL**, to be placed at the bottom of the vase, to purify the water.
- **SOIL** suitable for the type of plant. Often composed of a mixture of soil, peat, fertilizer, sand, and composted plants, it must provide nutrients, stimulate rooting, and retain water. It is essential for the development and growth of plants. There are different kinds depending on the stage of cuttings or repotting: potting soil, potting soil for flowering plants, for cacti, for succulents, repotting, etc.
  - ***Soil for seedlings and cuttings***: this is a very fine, light, and low-nutrient soil that is intended to retain moisture and heat and thus promote rooting.
  - ***General potting mix***: to be used when it is necessary to repot your existing plants. It is suitable for all house and flowering plants.
  - ***Indoor potting mix***: you can choose to repot your plants with this type of soil. It should be well-draining to avoid root suffocation, but sufficiently dense to maintain a good hold of the plant. It contains the essential nutrients for good development and harmonious growth.

- *Potting soil for cacti and succulents*: made up of sand and earth, this very light potting soil provides excellent water drainage, thus preventing your plants from rotting.
- *Soil for Mediterranean and citrus plants*: ultra-draining for these plants that cannot survive stagnant water, it is also enriched with nutrients for these very greedy plants.
- *Soil for aromatic plants*: best for plants generally grown for their leaves, its composition favors an abundant harvest.

• CLAY PELLETS, they are often forgotten, yet they can be helpful. They allow the water to drain, thus avoiding stagnation at the bottom of the pot that would cause the roots to rot. The majority of plants do not like having their roots in water! It is therefore ideal to put clay pellets or fine gravel at the bottom of the pot. You'll also want to make sure that your pots have holes in the bottom for drainage. If you opt for saucers, do not forget to empty them after each watering.

PILEA
PILEA

CHAPTER 1

Best practices

Propagate seeds, pits, and vegetable scraps

THE SEEDS AND PITS OF FRUITS AND VEGETABLES CAN GERMINATE TO BECOME NEW PLANTS OR TREES. THEIR GERMINATION IS NOT GUARANTEED: WITH THE NUMBER OF SEEDS IN AN APPLE OR ALL THE HAZELNUTS THAT FALL TO THE GROUND EACH YEAR, THE EARTH WOULD BE COVERED WITH TREES IF THEY ALL EMERGED!

THIS IS WHY WE ADVISE YOU TO SELECT SEVERAL TO INCREASE YOUR CHANCES OF SUCCESS. IT WILL THEN BE NECESSARY TO RESPECT THE TECHNIQUES SPECIFIC TO EACH SPECIES.

AND IF YOU WANT TO FIGHT AGAINST WASTE, DON'T THROW AWAY YOUR LEFT OVER VEGETABLES BECAUSE SOME CAN REGENERATE AND GROW BACK.

Pits and stones

Materials

- FRUIT PITS
- A GLASS CONTAINER
- A POT WITH DRAIN HOLE
- PAPER TOWEL OR ABSORBENT COTTON CLOTH
- ROOM TEMPERATURE WATER
- A 3–4 INCH POT WITH GOOD DRAINAGE
- SEEDLING MIX

Germinating pits and stones

1 Rinse your pits (large "seeds" from an avocado or mango for instance) with water using a small brush to clean them of residue. This avoids the risk of rot. Stones are found in fruits such as peaches, plums and cherries.

2 The pits will germinate on contact with water. Depending on the variety, they must be placed between two damp cotton balls, as is the case with mango, or on a perforated dish placed on a container filled with water, as with avocado. Hazelnuts and cherry stones, on the other hand, should be planted directly in soil.

Put the pits and stones in a pot, then in the ground

1 When the stones have germinated in water, you can put them in a pot filled with seed mix potting soil to help them gain strength. Be sure to keep the soil consistently moist and place them in a warm and bright place.

2 When the young shoots have reached 4 inches (10 cm) in height and the roots have developed well (they must be long and strong), you can put them in the ground. Be sure to do this in the spring, summer, or early fall.

Seeds and pips

Materials

- THE SEEDS OF A FRUIT OR VEGETABLE (APPLE, PEAR, ORANGE OR SQUASH)
- PAPER TOWEL OR ABSORBENT COTTON CLOTH
- ROOM-TEMPERATURE WATER
- A SMALL CONTAINER WITH A LID (POT OR RAMEQUIN)
- A 3–4 INCH POT WITH GOOD DRAINAGE
- SEEDLING MIX

Germinating seeds

1. To mitigate the risk of rot, rinse your seeds with water and clean off any residue. Some seeds, from citrus fruits for instance, are often referred to as pips.

2. Place them between two pieces of paper towel or cotton cloth moistened with warm water, then in a closed container, and place it in the refrigerator for three to six weeks. It is important to keep them in a cool place for some time to simulate the winter period they would experience in their natural state. This promotes germination as the seasons do!

3. As the weeks pass, make sure your substrate always stays moist.

Put the seeds in a pot, then in the ground

1. When your seeds have germinated, check that they have developed rootlets (very fine roots attached to the mother root) that show that they are robust.

2. Before planting them in the ground, it is recommended that you allow seedlings to develop in a pot for a while. The germinated seeds, still fragile, will grow their best if kept humid in a perforated pot filled with a seedling mix soil blend.

3. When the young shoot has reached about 4 inches (10 cm) and the roots are well developed (they must be long and robust) you can put them in the ground. Be sure you do this in the spring, summer, or early fall, though.

Vegetable scraps

Materials

- VEGETABLES SUITABLE FOR THIS TECHNIQUE (LEEKS, LETTUCE, CARROTS, SWEET POTATOES, POTATOES OR GARLIC)
- A GLASS CONTAINER (DISH, BOWL OR POT)
- A FUNNEL, OR NECK OF A PLASTIC BOTTLE
- ROOM-TEMPERATURE WATER

Which vegetables can regenerate?

All these foods—garlic, carrots, sweet potatoes, potatoes, leeks and lettuce—that we consume regularly can grow back ad infinitum.

All you have to do is collect the top or the bottom, depending on the vegetables, and soak them in water for a few weeks. Some vegetables can be eaten directly as they develop, such as leeks, lettuce, and even carrot tops. For others, like the carrot itself, the sweet potato or the potato, planting in the vegetable garden will be essential.

In this book you will find techniques adapted to carrots, sweet potatoes, leeks and lettuce, and you can also use them for other vegetables mentioned in the following pages.

NOTE

You can also regrow your aromatic herbs by placing a cutting in water (see pages 33–41).

Taking cuttings

PLACING A CUTTING IN A GLASS OF WATER ENCOURAGES IT TO TAKE ROOT AND IS ONE OF THE EASIEST WAYS TO MULTIPLY YOUR FAVORITE PLANTS.
THIS METHOD HAS A HIGH RATE OF SUCCESS AND ALLOWS YOU TO MONITOR THE DEVELOPMENT OF ROOTS IN REAL TIME. THERE ARE SEVERAL METHODS OF ROOTING CUTTINGS IN SOIL OR IN WATER DEPENDING ON THE TYPE OF PLANT: A STEM, LEAF OR ROOTS, WHICH ARE TAKEN FROM THE MOTHER PLANT, OR A BRANCH THAT IS TAKEN FROM A CUTTING BEFORE DETACHING IT, IN THE CASE OF LAYERING. SOME PLANTS TEND TO CAST OFF “PUPS” OR “OFFSETS” THAT ARE WELL-SUITED TO PROPAGATION.

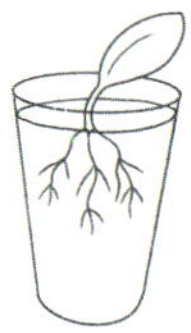

Starting cuttings in water

Materials

- A CUTTING TAKEN FROM THE MOTHER PLANT
- A CLEAN PAIR OF PRUNING SHEARS OR SCISSORS, DISINFECTED WITH ALCOHOL
- GLASS CONTAINER (JAR OR VASE)
- A FUNNEL OR NECK OF A PLASTIC BOTTLE
- ROOM-TEMPERATURE WATER
- SEEDLING MIX FOR PLANTING AFTER PROPAGATION IN WATER

The limits of the method and how to circumvent them

This method is simple, but it has its limitations. Sometimes the roots of the cutting acclimatize to the aquatic environment. Thus, when they are put back in the ground, they don't adapt well. To avoid this problem, plant the stem in the ground as soon as small white bumps appear, which mark the beginning of future roots. It is also advisable to choose a light soil so that the cutting adapts more easily and more quickly to its new soil and its new growing conditions.

Note that it is also possible to keep the cuttings in water for many years. Adapted to their new aquatic environment, the plants evolve in the water without difficulty. Maintenance consists only of changing the water from time to time, and the decorative effect can be excellent!

When to put a cutting in water?

Indoor plants can be cut year-round. However, it is preferable to make your cuttings when the plant is growing in order to facilitate the recovery of the cutting. The growing period extends from the end of February to the end of August.

For outdoor plants, it's the same principle. Cuttings are made from spring until the end of summer.

Materials

- A MOTHER PLANT IN EXCELLENT HEALTH FROM WHICH YOUR CUTTING CAN BE TAKEN
- A CLEAN PAIR OF PRUNING SHEARS OR SCISSORS, DISINFECTED WITH ALCOHOL
- A TRANSPARENT CONTAINER SO THAT YOU CAN SEE THE ROOTS GROW!
- A FUNNEL OR NECK OF A PLASTIC BOTTLE, WHICH WILL KEEP THE TOP OF THE CUTTING OUT OF THE WATER
- WATER, PREFERABLY RAINWATER
- A PIECE OF CHARCOAL (OPTIONAL)
- SEEDLING MIX FOR PLANTING AFTER PROPAGATING IN WATER

Preparing the cutting

It is important to choose a healthy stem without flowers but with well developed leaves. It must be free of disease, injury, and insects. The cutting will draw its energy and its reserves from its leaves. Thus the more they are developed, the more they are able to provide everything that is necessary for the development of the cutting.

Cut a stem of about 6 inches (15 cm) using a clean pruner, just below a node, where the buds form. Only this area can send out new roots. The cut must be made at an angle to prevent the water from stagnating in the cut of the mother plant. If you don't have pruners, use a pair of scissors if necessary, but never cut by hand.

Remove the leaves from the stem to keep only three, on the upper part. If there is one, remove the terminal bud. The plant will thus concentrate its energy on the development of the roots.

What's the best water to use?

It is ideal to use soft water (rainwater, river water) to fill your container, because plants are less fond of tap water, which is often treated with chlorine and can contain minerals. Make sure the water is at room temperature. You can place a piece of charcoal in the container: this natural product prevents root rot. Soft water and charcoal make it possible to change the water less often.

DON'T PANIC

It's not always easy to get fresh rainwater or charcoal, but do not panic! This will not prevent you from propagating cuttings. On the other hand, you should remember to change the water more frequently—at least once a week.

Finding the best location

Find a bright location for your cutting, out of direct sunlight so that the leaves do not dry out and so as not to interfere with the proper development of the roots. Avoid as much as possible placing it too close to a so-called "dry" heat source, such as radiators and fireplaces. To promote its development, your cutting needs a humid and warm environment, at around 65°F (19°C), and shelter from drafts.

From now on, arm yourself with patience and watch for the appearance of the first roots!

Repotting the cutting

When the roots are about an inch (2.5 cm) long it is essential to place the cutting in the ground so that the roots quickly and easily adapt to their new natural element and strengthen.

1. Use a pot about 4 inches (10 cm) in diameter. Fill it with seedling soil: a light, fine and well-draining soil. This is the ideal type of soil for promoting roots on your tender cutting.

2. Make a hole in the soil to so that you can gently slip the cutting in without damaging the roots. Then gently pack the soil around the cutting.

3. Water regularly to keep the soil moist and watch for signs of growth, such as new leaves and elongation of the stem.

Establishing cuttings in soil

Materials

- A MOTHER PLANT IN EXCELLENT HEALTH
- A CLEAN PAIR OF PRUNING SHEARS OR SCISSORS, DISINFECTED
- A SHARP THIN KNIFE FOR SUCCULENTS AND CACTUS PADDLES
- A POT WITH HOLES THAT WILL ALLOW THE WATER TO ESCAPE, 3–4 INCHES (8–10 CM) IN DIAMETER
- CLAY PELLETS OR GRAVEL TO ENSURE PROPER WATER DRAINAGE
- A GLASS OR CLEAR PLASTIC BELL (BOTTLE CUT IN TWO)
- FOR SUCCULENTS AND CACTI: LIGHT SOIL COMPOSED OF PEAT AND SAND
- FOR HOUSE PLANTS: SEEDLING MIX OR GOOD QUALITY POTTING SOIL
- RAINWATER

Which plant to use?

Cuttings can be made from stems, leaves, or roots. The fragment you choose depends on the type of plant from which you want to take cuttings. Thus, cutting a stem is suitable for all plants that produce one. Some only produce leaves, such as the varieties of crassulas, echeveria, begonias, sansevierias, or peperomias. Finally, you can also take root cuttings, but this technique is particularly difficult, and the chances of success are quite slim. This concerns perennials such as thistle, raspberry, aralia, etc.

In this book we will explore the simplest technique—that of stems and leaves. For now let's leave root cuttings to the professionals!

Prepare the pot for your cutting

Regardless of the container that will accommodate your cutting, it can be a clay pot or a plastic pot (a yogurt container, for example). Two things are important:
- It must have a hole (or three) at the bottom for good drainage,
- It should not be too large: 3–4 inches (7–10 cm). The roots will develop better in a small pot to start.

First, place gravel or clay pebbles in your container about 1 inch (2 cm) deep, which will allow the water to drain properly. Then pour in the soil, wetting it and letting the water drain well. Finally, make a hole in the soil in the middle, using a pencil.

NOTE

For cactus and succulent leaf cuttings: *do not wet the soil before placing the leaves. These plants do not need moisture to grow. Place them directly in dry soil.*

Leaf cuttings

Materials

- HEALTHY LEAVES TAKEN FROM THE MOTHER PLANT
- CLEAN SHEARS OR SCISSORS, DISINFECTED WITH ALCOHOL
- A SHARP KNIFE OR RAZOR
- A 3–4 INCH (8–10 CM) POT WITH GOOD DRAINAGE
- CLAY PELLETS OR GRAVEL TO ENSURE PROPER DRAINAGE
- PLASTIC WRAP

What plants to start from a leaf cutting?

A new plant from a simple leaf... an almost magical technique! It is not the most common, but for some plants it is the only one that will allow you to make cuttings. This is the case of the following plants—kalanchoë, opuntia, echeveria, sempervivum, sedum, crassula, yucca, mother-in-law's tongue, begonia, peperomia—because they have leaves that produce small roots in contact with the ground.

What time of year?

These leaf cuttings are done year-round, except during the frost period. But the ideal periods are spring and summer especially because the heat ensures the cutting will take well. Beware of excess water—cacti and crassulas need dry soil, begonias and peperomia require slightly damp soil to grow properly.

Preparing the cutting and putting it in the soil

Begonias and Peperomias

Detach a healthy leaf with a petiole (small stem that connects the leaf to the main stem of the plant): cut it about 1 inch (3 cm) from the base of the leaf.

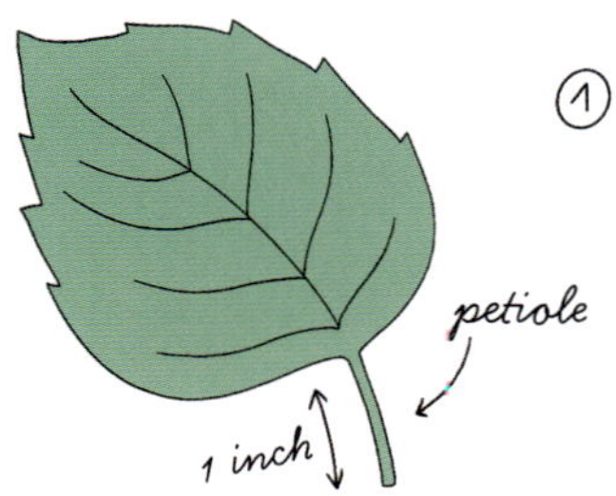

Using a fine blade, make a ½ inch (1 cm) incision across the largest veins on the back of the leaf and make the cuts at the intersection with the main lateral vein. The young shoots will develop at these incision points, marking the beginning of propagation, and therefore, of new plants!

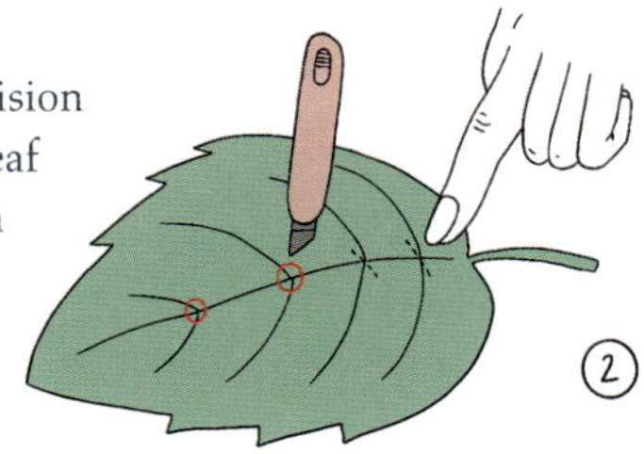

Prepare your pot by placing clay pellets in the bottom, then a good-quality seedling soil mix. Push the petiole into the hole and lay the leaf on the moist potting soil with the notches on the bottom (soil side). Keep the leaf flat and in contact with the soil by placing small pebbles on its edges.

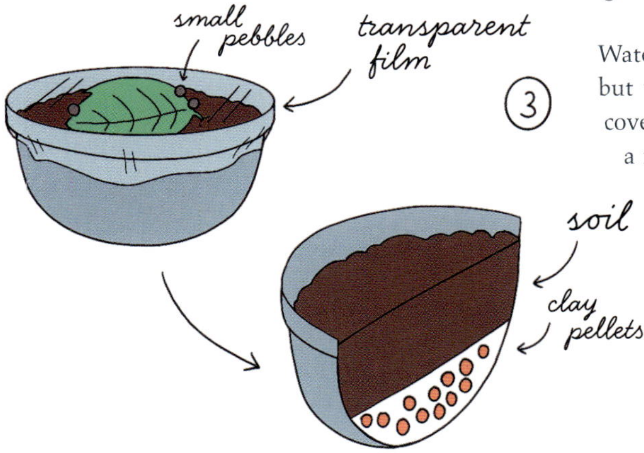

Water regularly to keep the soil slightly moist, but without wetting the leaves. You can also cover the planter with plastic wrap: this creates a mini greenhouse and maintains humidity at close to 100 percent. This is called the "smothered cutting". Place your pot in a warm room, ideally 68°F–75°F (20°C–24°C). The room should be well-lit but without direct sunlight. New plantlets should appear between three to six weeks later depending on the species.

Leaf cuttings for succulents and cacti

Take a healthy leaf by breaking it off of the base of the plant. For cacti with thick trunks or snowshoes (opuntia, for example), take a knife without teeth and cut the part to be cut cleanly. Leave it to dry for three to four days; this allows the "wound" to heal (for cacti, the drying period can be longer, two to three weeks, depending on the size of the cutting).

By the time a callus (scarring) forms your cutting is ready to be planted! You can then plant the base of the leaf in the ground. It doesn't have to be pushed in too much. Once in the ground, do not water; you will do so only when you see small roots appear, with very little water. If the soil is too wet, the cutting may rot quickly.

Cuttings from stems

Materials

- HEALTHY SHOOTS TAKEN FROM THE MOTHER PLANT
- CLEAN SHEARS OR SCISSORS, DISINFECTED WITH ALCOHOL
- A CLEAR GLASS VASE OR A WELL DRAINED POT
- A CLEAR GLASS CLOCHE OR A PLASTIC BOTTLE CUT IN HALF

Which plants, and when?

Cuttings from a stem can be made in different ways, in soil or in water, depending on the plants and the season. Porcelain flower, rubber, mosaic plant, sleeper plant, pachira, crow's feet, and misery can be cut using these two techniques. A stem is usually taken from them in the spring through early fall, while the plant is actively growing. They can sometimes be enclosed in a transparent cover to recreate the conditions of a mini greenhouse, which is called the smothered cutting.

Taking the cutting and preparing the soil

The sample is identical to that of the cutting in water: choose a healthy stem, with at least three leaves. Identify the node of the stem from which you wish to take a cutting and using clean shears, cut a stem of about 6 inches (15 cm). Make sure you always cut on the bias. Do not forget to remove the leaves to keep only two or three well developed, on the upper part of the stem.

Prepare the pot of soil, make a hole in the middle, and push the stem into the hole. Gently tamp down the soil around the cutting.

What is the best environment?

You can then water to moisten the soil well. By placing the pot under a glass bell (cloche) or the bottom of a plastic bottle that has been cut in half, you'll create a mini greenhouse and will keep the cutting hydrated with a humidity level close to 100%. Then put the pot in a bright and warm place at a temperature of about 68°F–75°F (20°C–24°C). Water again as soon as the soil dries on the surface.

As soon as the first roots appear, after a month to a month and a half, remove the bell.

Cuttings by layering

Materials

- A MOTHER PLANT
- PINS
- A 3–4 INCH POT WITH DRAINAGE HOLES IN THE BOTTOM
- CLAY PELLETS OR GRAVEL TO ENSURE PROPER DRAINAGE
- SUITABLE POTTING SOIL MIX

Which plants and when?

This cutting technique is mainly used for climbing and drooping plants or those that produce aerial roots. Chain of hearts, porcelain flower, and philodendron are taken using the cuttings by layering technique. The ideal period is from spring to mid-autumn, while the plant is growing.

Taking the cutting and preparing the soil

This very simple technique consists of burying a portion of stem in a second pot and keeping it in the ground using pins or even a simple pebble, without separating it from the mother plant. This allows you to create a new plant without cutting stems.

Choose a supple and healthy rooting stem: it must have an aerial root. The soil used to propagate it must be rich and moist. Push the future root into the ground. Then secure the stem with pins to prevent it from moving.

Water to keep the soil moist until the root system develops after about four weeks. At this point, you can separate the stem from the mother plant by cutting it with pruning shears as close as possible to the cutting. Keep watering afterwards!

Separating an offset

Materials

- AN "OFFSET" WITH ROOTS
- A WELL DRAINED POT APPROPRIATELY SIZED FOR YOUR OFFSET
- CLAY PELLETS OR GRAVEL TO ENSURE PROPER DRAINAGE
- SEEDLING SOIL MIX

What is an offset?

An offset is a new shoot with leaves (like a mini plant, which often grows at the edge of the pot or next to the parent plant in the wild) and can be taken out to make a new, separate plant. Offsets are sometimes referred to as a sucker, or a pup.

Which plants and when?

The following plants—elephant ear, Chinese money plant, banana tree, false philodendron, bird of paradise, and aloe vera—are propagated from an offset. The separation of the offset is best practiced from spring to mid-autumn, during the plant's growing period.

Potting up the offset

Unpot the plant to be divided and carefully remove the soil surrounding the pup by hand. Retain the maximum amount of roots, which will give the plant a greater chance of recovery. Then, put it in a pot with holes filled with clay pebbles at the bottom and seedling soil on top. Water regularly to keep the soil moist and place your cutting in a bright, heated room between 65°F–70°F (18°C–21°C).

NOTE

Be patient, it may take three or four weeks before you see signs of a new leaf—a sign that your cutting has taken!

Chapter 2

Edible plants

Ocimum basilicum

Basil

SAME TECHNIQUE
Sage

IF THERE IS AN ESSENTIAL FLAVOR IN THE KITCHEN, IT IS BASIL! ITS FRESH SCENT IS USEFUL IN MANY MEDITERRANEAN RECIPES. IT'S EASY TO GROW FROM CUTTINGS SO YOU CAN HAVE IT YEAR-ROUND!

Family: Lamiaceae
Origin: Southeast Asia
Best time to take cuttings: year-round
Root a stem cutting in water, then in soil

Plant care

- **EXPOSURE**
Shaded; avoid direct sunlight, especially in summer. Also, keep from drafts and overheated areas.
- **WATERING**
In a small pot, the soil can dry out quickly; in spring and summer you'll probably need to water 2 or 3 times a week to keep the soil moist. Avoid wetting the leaves as it can promote mold and pests.
- **POTTING**
Basil is an "annual" and tends to die off in the fall.

1 Take cuttings of healthy top growth tips about 3 to 4 inches (8 to 10 cm) long. Remove the basal leaves (leaves lowest on the stem), keeping only three to four smaller ones at the top.

2 Drop your cuttings into a glass container, making sure to keep the leaves out of the water.

3 As soon as the roots appear, in about two to three weeks, repot the cuttings in a 4-inch pot. For best results use seedling soil with clay pellets at the bottom and put three cuttings in each pot. Place your newly potted cuttings in a warm, bright room with temperatures between 55°F–70°F (12°C–20°C), or outside if temperatures allow.

4 Water regularly to keep the soil moist.

You may begin harvesting your basil leaves as soon as your plants are leafy and 4 to 6 inches tall (10 to 15 cm).

Coriandrum sativum

Coriander

CORIANDER IS ONE OF THE MOST AROMATIC HERBS YOU CAN GROW. THIS FRAGRANT, LEAFY GREEN IS WIDELY USED IN SALADS, SOUPS, ENTREES AND SAUCES.

Family: Apiaceae
Origin: Asia
Best time to take cuttings: spring or summer, while the plant is growing quickly.
A STEM CUTTING WILL TAKE ROOT IN WATER OR SOIL.

Plant care

• **EXPOSURE**
Part shade, or well lit, but sheltered from the hottest summer sun.

• **WATERING/MAINTENANCE**
In a small pot, the soil dries out very quickly, so be sure to keep it moist.
– In spring and summer, water regularly, 2 to 3 times a week depending on the temperature. Avoid wetting the leaves as this can promote mold and pests.
– In winter, let nature take its course! But if it does not rain for several weeks, give it a little water.

• **POTTING**
Repot once a year in a well-drained pot that's an inch or two (2–4cm) bigger.

Rooting cuttings in water

1. Take cuttings from young stems, about 3 inches long. Cut just below a node. Remove lower (basal) leaves, keeping just four or five at the top.

2. Place your cuttings in a glass container, keeping the leaves out of the water.

3. As soon as the roots appear, after three to four weeks, place them in a 4-inch (10 cm) diameter pot with seedling soil. Place the pots in a bright, heated room between 55°F–70°F (12°C–20°C).

4. Wait six weeks for roots to develop, then repot in regular potting soil. Next spring you can plant them in the ground!

Starting your cuttings in water ensures that the roots will grow well.

Rooting cuttings in soil

1. Take cuttings from young stems, about 3 inches long. Cut just below a node. Remove lower basal leaves, keeping just 4 or 5 at the top.

2. Prepare a very small pot about 2 to 3 inches (8 cm) with clay pellets at the bottom and filled with seedling soil. Poke small holes in the soil, gently plant your cuttings in the holes, and then water them in.

3. Place the pots in a bright, heated room between 55°F–70°F (12°C–20°C). Wait two to four weeks for roots to develop.

4. Once they have rooted you can repot them in a pot that's an inch or two larger, then plant them in the ground next spring.

Initially, before taking stem cuttings from coriander, you'll want to wait until the mother plant is 5 or 6 inches (12 or 15 cm) tall and is leafy and well developed.

Mentha

Mint

ONE OF THE FRESHEST AROMATIC HERBS—ITS PERFUME IS AN EXCITING TONIC!

Family: Lamiaceae
Origin: Europe
Best time to take cuttings: spring and summer while the plant is actively growing.
TAKES ROOT IN BOTH SOIL AND WATER.

Plant care

- **EXPOSURE**
Part shade or lots of light but protect from full summer sun until well established.
- **WATERING / PRUNING**
In a small pot the soil dries out quickly, so be sure to keep it moist – Water 2 to 3 times a week in spring and summer. Avoid wetting the leaves as much as possible. Prune back after flowering.
-In winter, let nature take its course! But if it does not rain for several weeks, give it a little water.
- **POTTING**
Repot once a year in a well-drained pot that's an inch or two (2–4 cm) bigger.

Rooting cuttings in water

1. Cut young mint stalks about 3 inches (8 cm) long. Cut under a node. Remove the basal leaves, keeping only four or five at the top of the stem.

2. Place your cuttings in a glass container, keeping the leaves out of the water.

3. As soon as roots start to appear about three to four weeks later, repot your cuttings in a 4-inch (10 cm) pot, filled with seedling soil. Keep them in a bright, heated room between 55°F–70°F (12°C–20°C).

4. Wait six weeks for roots to develop, then repot in regular potting soil. Next spring you can plant them in the ground!

Rooting cuttings in soil

1. Take cuttings from young stems, about 3 inches long. Cut just below a node. Remove lower basal leaves, keeping just four or five at the top.

2. Fill some 3-inch (6 cm) pots with seedling soil, make a hole in the soil for each cutting and gently water them in. Place your pots in a heated room that's ideally between 65°F–70°F (18°C–21°C).

3. After giving the roots two to three weeks to develop, you can then repot them in a pot that's about 1 or 2 inches (2 to 5 cm) larger (only one cutting per pot as mint has an extremely vigorous root system).

Rosemary

AN ESSENTIAL FOR THE KITCHEN! ROSEMARY IS ALSO TOUTED FOR ITS HEALTH BENEFITS AS A SLEEP AND DIGESTIVE AID.

Family: Lamiaceae
Origin: Mediterranean Basin
Best time to take cuttings: spring, summer, during the active growing season.
TAKES ROOT IN WATER OR SOIL

Plant care

- **EXPOSURE**
Sunny, but with some protection from full burning sun.
- **WATERING**
In a small pot the soil dries out quickly, so be sure to keep it moist.
– In spring and summer, water regularly 2 to 3 times a week, depending on the temperature.
– Water very little in the winter unless there's a dry spell.
- **POTTING**
Repot once a year (in the fall or spring) in a well-drained pot that's an inch or two (2-4 cm) bigger.

Rooting cuttings in water

1. Cut flexible shoots (avoid woody stalks) about 3 inches (8 cm) long. Cut under a node. Remove any leaves on the first couple inches of the cuttings.

2. Place your cuttings in a glass container and arrange them so that the leaves stay out of the water.

3. As soon as roots start to appear about three to four weeks later, repot your cuttings in a 4-inch (10 cm) pot, filled with seedling soil. Keep them in a bright, heated room between 55°F–70°F (12°C–20°C).

4. Wait six weeks for roots to develop, then repot in regular potting soil. Next spring you can plant them in the ground!

Rooting cuttings in soil

1. Take cuttings from young stems, about 3 inches long. Cut just below a node. Remove any leaves on the first couple inches of the cuttings.

2. Fill a small 3-inch (6 cm) pot with seedling soil, make small holes to place your cuttings in and gently water in the cuttings.

3. Place your pots in a heated room that's ideally between 65°F–70°F (18°C–21°C).

4. Wait about two to four weeks for roots to develop.

5. Once your cuttings have shown signs of new growth you can repot them in slightly larger pot filled with regular potting soil.

Thymus

Thyme

ITS AROMA TAKES US DIRECTLY TO PROVENCE! IDEAL FOR FLAVORING MEAT AND FISH, IT IS ALSO USED TO AUGMENT SOUPS AND SAUCES.

Family: Lamiaceae
Origin: Mediterranean Basin
Best time to take cuttings: spring and summer during the plant's vigorous growth.
LATERAL SHOOTS TAKE ROOT IN THE GROUND WHEN BURIED

Plant care

- **EXPOSURE**
Sunny.
- **WATERING / PRUNING**
Make sure to keep the soil moist as your small pot will dry out quickly.
– Water 2 to 3 times a week in spring and summer. Avoid wetting the leaves as much as possible. Prune back after flowering.
– In winter, let nature take its course! But if it does not rain for several weeks, give it a little water.
- **POTTING**
Repot every year in spring or autumn, always in a well-drained pot about an inch or two (2-5 cm) larger.

1. Using pruning shears, cut off several 3-inch (8 cm) sprigs of thyme. Remove the small leaves at the base of the stems.

2. Fill a small 2½-to-3-inch (6 cm) pot with seedling soil. Poke several holes in the soil and place at least three cuttings in the pot. Place the pot on a saucer or in a container and pour water into the container so that your cuttings can "drink" from the bottom while the leaves stay dry.

3. Cover everything with a glass or plastic bell to create a mini greenhouse to keep the heat and humidity elevated. Place the pot in a bright place with indirect light, ideally in a room that's between 65°F–70°F (18°C–21°C).

4. Wait about ten days for some roots to develop. You may then remove the bell and plant the thyme in the garden or in a larger pot.

Once your thyme thickens up and reaches 4 to 6 inches (10 to 12 cm) you can harvest as needed.

Ananas Comosus

Pineapple

AFTER ENJOYING A PINEAPPLE, KEEP THE TOP! ITS A FAIRLY EASY CUTTING TO ROOT AND WILL MAKE A PRETTY PLANT WITH LONG SWORD-SHAPED LEAVES.

Family: Bromeliaceae
Origin: Brazil
Best time to take a cutting: spring or summer
ROOTS IN WATER

Plant care

- **EXPOSURE**
Bright but without direct sun. Keep away from sources of dry heat such as radiators.
- **WATERING**
Soil should be kept moist.
– In summer water 2 to 3 times a week
– In winter, once a week, making sure the soil dries between the two waterings. Place the pot on a saucer filled with fine gravel with a small amount of water or wet clay pellets to keep the humidity up.
- **POTTING**
Pineapples produce few roots, it's not necessary to repot every year. However, you may want to repot to recover its offsets so that you can propagate them.

1 Using a sharp clean knife cut off the top of a pineapple 1 inch (2 to 3 cm) below its leaves.

2 Place the pineapple top in a jar or glass of water so that only the fleshy part is submerged, taking care that the leaves are not in the water. Place the cutting in a well-lit room with the temperature around 65°F–68°F (18°C–20°C). Change the water once a week.

3 Roots should begin to grow within four to six weeks.

4 Once the roots are about an inch long (2 to 3 cm) you can repot your cutting in a pot with a diameter that's a bit bigger than the pineapple top. Use a potting bromeliad specific potting soil (orchid mix will do in a pinch).

You will be lucky to get a fruit on your plant if you don't live in a tropical area or aren't able to grow in a greenhouse, however it is possible in temperate regions with hot humid summers!

Cut the head of your pineapple about an inch (2-3cm) below the leaves.

Persea americana

Avocado

THE AVOCADO'S NATIVE ENVIRONMENT IS WARM AND MOSTLY FROST FREE. HOWEVER, SINCE AVOCADO PITS ARE EASY TO GERMINATE IT'S A FUN PLANT TO GROW INDOORS.

Family: Lauraceae
Origin: Central America
Best time to propagate: year-round
BEST TO ROOT IN WATER INITIALLY

Plant care

- **EXPOSURE**
Bright and dry while avoiding direct sunlight.
- **WATERING**
Make sure to keep the soil moist:
– Once or twice a week in winter
– 2 or 3 times a week in the warmer months
- **POTTING**
Repot every 2 to 3 years in the spring.

1 Collect your avocado pit and let it soak in hot water for 30 minutes. Then let it dry for three days.

2 Place a plastic cup with a large hole in a glass of water and put the pit on the hole with its tip up and its base submerged in the water. Another method is to poke three toothpicks into the pit so as to suspend it only partly in the glass of water. Place the pit in a bright room, out of direct sunlight at around 70°C (20°F). Change the water once a week.

3 Wait two to three weeks until you see the pit crack, the first roots sprout and the stem begins to grow. You can then plant it in a pot that's about 4 inches (10 cm) in diameter filled with seedling soil. Make a hole in the soil and gently slip the pit's roots into the hole without damaging them. Then cover by packing the soil lightly around the stem and water it in.

4 Water regularly to keep the soil moist and watch for signs of development, mainly new leaves and elongation of the stem.

If you live in a zone with little or no frost your avocado tree may start to bear fruit in four to five years. You will need to grow a couple varieties to get them to pollinate and bear fruit.

Musa

Banana

SAME TECHNIQUE
Bird of paradise

SOME PLANTS SUMMON FAR-OFF LANDS, AND THE BANANA IS ONE OF THEM! THOUGH IT APPEARS TO HAVE A TRUNK LIKE A TYPICAL TREE, IT IS ACTUALLY A LARGE HERBACEOUS PLANT. IT SPREADS BY UNDERGROUND STEMS THAT PRODUCE ROOTS, OTHERWISE KNOWN AS RHIZOMES.

Family: Musaceae
Origin: West Indies, Asia, Australia
Best time to propagate: the heat of spring and summer will give your plants the best chance of success
TAKES ROOT IN THE GROUND FROM A SPROUT

Plant care

- **EXPOSURE**
Bright indirect light, around 68°F–72°F (18°C–22°C).
- **WATERING**
Mist the foliage daily with fresh water.
– In spring and summer, water twice a week, allowing the surface to dry between the two waterings.
– In winter, water less often, allowing the soil to dry to a depth of an inch (2–3 cm) before watering again. Keep away from heat sources that can dry out the foliage.
- **NUTRIENTS**
Feed your banana liquid fertilizer every couple weeks during the growing season (Mar–Sept).
- **POTTING**
Repot every 2 to 3 years in the spring.

1. You'll need a mother plant as source material. Look for offsets, or "suckers" around the base of the plant and gently remove the soil around them.

2. Choose shoots composed of at least 4 or 5 leaves and be sure to keep a rhizome (underground root) intact. Eliminate lower leaves, keeping only the younger ones.

3. Place each sprout in a well-drained pot filled with seedling soil with clay pellets at the bottom. Keep your "starts" in a bright room around 70°F (20°C).

4. Water regularly so that the soil is always a little moist.

5. When you see a new leaf poking up, it's a sign that your cutting has taken.

Citrus x limon

Lemon

SAME TECHNIQUE
Kumquat, orange, grapefruit

SEEDS FROM YOUR LEMONS, LIMES OR ORANGES CAN BE GERMINATED INTO BEAUTIFUL TREES.

Family: Rutaceae
Origin: Southeast Asia
Best time to germinate: year-round
CITRUS SEEDS (ALSO KNOWN AS PIPS) NEED A LOT OF MOISTURE TO GERMINATE

Plant care

• EXPOSURE
Sunny. Full sun is very important for flowering and production of lemons. Citrus trees cannot handle frost. In the winter, a veranda or cool room with temperatures between 40°F–50°F (5°C–10°C) will work!

• WATERING
– In spring and summer water your lemon 2–3 times a week, a little more during very hot weather.
– In winter, let the soil dry out on the surface, water approximately every ten days.

• NUTRIENTS
Feed your tree with citrus fertilizer, monthly, April through September.

• POTTING
Repot in the spring, every three years using citrus soil.

1 Collect about ten pips to maximize your chances of success. Soak them in water for twenty-four hours to clean them of residue.

2 Sandwich the pips between two pieces of cotton or paper towels dampened with lukewarm water. Then keep them in an airtight bag in a warm place for 2 to 3 weeks.

3 When the seeds have germinated, place them in a cup or container of water. The germinated seeds must soak in the water. Wait and watch them grow!

4 When the stems have reached 6 inches (15 cm) and have developed two or three leaves, it's time to put them in the ground. Prepare well-drained, 4-inch (10 cm) pots with clay pellets at the bottom and seedling soil on top. Gently bury your sprouts, without damaging the roots. Place the pots in the sun and keep the soil moist.

It will take seven or eight years for your citrus trees to produce their first fruits.

Mangifera indica

Mango

THIS EXOTIC TREE PRODUCES DELICIOUS VITAMIN-PACKED FRUITS. IT CAN BE GROWN IN THE GROUND IN TROPICAL REGIONS. ELSEWHERE, KEEP IT IN A POT SO THAT YOU CAN BRING IT IN FROM THE COLD IN WINTER.

Family: Anacardiaceae
Origin: India, Burma
Best time to propagate: year-round
Requires a lot of moisture to root before being planted in soil

Plant care

• **EXPOSURE**
Sunny, avoiding the scorching summer sun.
• **WATERING**
Make sure to keep the soil moist:
– Once or twice a week in winter
– 2 to 3 times a week in the hot season.
Keep away from sources of dry heat like radiators. Set the pot on a saucer with wet clay pellets or gravel. Evaporation will humidify the surrounding air.
Mist the foliage several times a week, preferably with rainwater.
• **POTTING**
Repot every 2 or 3 years in the spring.

1 Collect the pit of a mango. Let it dry for a few days. When the pit and pulpy remains are very dry, you can delicately extract the almond shaped seed which is at the heart. Check that it looks healthy and shows no signs of mold.

2 Place a couple of layers paper towels in a bowl, place the seed on them and then cover with a few more layers, enough that the seed will be protected from light. Dampen the paper towels and put them under a glass or a plastic bell to create a mini greenhouse.

3 Place the seed in a dark room at a temperature of 65°F–68°F (18°C–20°C). Take the bell or covering off every day for a few minutes to let it air out.

4 When the seed has germinated in about fifteen days, it's time to put it in soil. Fill a 6-inch pot almost to the top with seedling soil, then place the seed on top, gently burying only the root. Make sure the root is completely covered, but do not bury the seed.

5 Water regularly to keep the soil moist and watch for signs of development. The stem should start to form and elongate, and new leaves should start in about two weeks.

You will probably be able to repot about a month later.

Corylus avellana

Hazelnut

A SYMBOL OF WISDOM AND JUSTICE, THE HAZELNUT IS A RUSTIC TREE THAT YOU WILL SEE THROUGHOUT EUROPE. HAZELNUTS ARE HIGHLY NUTRITIOUS AND VERY TASTY TOO!

Family: Betulaceae
Origin: temperate regions of the northern hemisphere
Best time to propagate: September
Roots directly in soil

Plant care

• **EXPOSURE**
Sunny, sheltered from the wind and scorching summer sun.

• **WATERING**
Make sure to keep the soil moist:
– Once or twice a week, even more when it's hot.
– In winter, let nature take its course! Water only if it does not rain for several weeks in a row.

• **PLANTING**
Plant in autumn. Hazelnut trees can live in pots for several years, but then they must be planted in the ground. Plant several to promote pollination.

1 Collect hazelnuts directly from trees if possible. You will want to plant several to increase chances of success, and ideally two different varieties to promote fertilization and therefore the production of hazelnuts. Save the shells.

2 Fill 3-inch (6 cm) pots with seedling soil. Half bury the hazelnuts and then cover the surface with gravel. Place your pots outside in a sheltered area.

3 Water them regularly, keeping the soil slightly moist. Beware of oversaturation and excess water that will rot the hazelnuts.

4 You'll need to patiently wait until spring for the hazelnuts to germinate.

Your hazelnut tree will need another three or four years to produce nuts.

Olive

Olea europea

A SYMBOL OF SUN AND HEAT, BUT ALSO OF PEACE AND STRENGTH, THE OLIVE TREE HAS ALWAYS BEEN APPRECIATED FOR ITS LUSTROUS GREEN FOLIAGE. THIS PLANT IS A PERFECT SCREEN OR BACKDROP FOR YOUR BALCONY OR TERRACE.

Family: Oleaceae
Origin: Mediterranean region
Best time to take a cutting: summer
TAKES ROOT IN SOIL, FROM A BRANCH

Plant care

- **EXPOSURE**

Bright, without direct sun. Protect it from freezing in winter with a frost covering.

- **WATERING / PRUNING**

– In spring and summer, water regularly 2 to 3 times a week depending on the heat.
– In winter, let nature take its course! But if it does not rain for several weeks, water a little.
– At the end of winter and at the beginning of spring, prune it by cutting the branches that have grown at its foot or along its trunk. Also cut the branches that tend towards the ground and those that grow inward.

- **POTTING**

In the spring, every 2 or 3 years in a well-drained soil.

1 Take a young new shoot 6 inches (15 cm) long. It should be young and supple, but the base should have a little stiffness. Cut just under a node, then remove all the leaves to keep only five or six at the end. Using a sharp knife or pruning shears, peel off a piece of bark, at the base of the stem, 2 to 3 cm long.

2 In a pot filled with seedling soil, make a hole, and plant the cutting. Pack the soil well around the stem. Water well to moisten the soil. Place a glass or plastic cloche over the pot, to create a greenhouse effect.

3 Place the pot in a bright and warm place (between 65°F–70°F/18°C–21°C) and water as soon as the soil dries on the surface.

4 Wait about eight weeks before the roots develop. You can then remove the bell and continue growing in pots until next spring.

5 Then you will repot your small olive tree, or you will plant it in the ground with a well-drained potting soil.

Citrus sinensis

Orange

IF YOU LIVE IN A WARM CLIMATE YOU CAN PLANT YOUR ORANGE TREE IN THE GROUND. IN TEMPERATE CLIMATES YOU WILL NEED TO KEEP IT IN A POT AND BRING IT INSIDE DURING THE WINTER.

Family: Rutaceae
Origin: Asia
Best time to germinate: year-round
Seeds germinate best with a lot of moisture

Plant care

• **EXPOSURE**
Sunny. The sun is very important, as it promotes flowering and therefore the production of oranges. The orange tree fears frost. In winter, put it in a veranda or a cool room between 41°F–50°F (5°C–10°C).

• **WATERING**
– In spring and summer, water it about 2 to 3 times a week, a little more when the days are very hot.
– In winter, let the soil dry out on the surface, water approximately every ten days.

• **NUTRIENTS**
Apply citrus fertilizer all the months, from April to the end of September.

• **POTTING**
In the spring, every three years, with citrus soil.

1 Collect about ten pips (seeds) to maximize your chances of success. Soak them in water for twenty-four hours to clean them of any residue.

2 Choose pots 4 inches (10 cm) in diameter, line them with clay pebbles at the bottom, then pour in seedling soil. Water the soil and plant three seeds about half an inch (1 cm) deep in each pot. Arrange a glass or plastic bell jar over the pot to create a greenhouse effect, which will facilitate the germination of seeds.

3 Place the pots in a bright room, without direct sunlight, and heated between 65°F–70°F (18°C–21°C). Keep the soil moist. Wait two to four weeks before seeing the young shoots develop!

4 When the sprouts are 2 to 4 inches (5-10 cm) tall and have 2-3 leaves, remove the bell and replant each sprout in an individual pot. Place them in the light and continue watering.

Wait seven to eight years before your orange tree produces its first fruits.

Apple

Malus

IN THE GROUND, IN A GARDEN OR IN A POT ON A BALCONY—WHAT IF YOU TRY TO GROW A BEAUTIFUL APPLE TREE FROM A SEED?

Family: Rosaceae
Origin: Kazakhstan
Best time to germinate: year-round
Germinate the seeds in water

Plant care

• **EXPOSURE**
Sunny. Full sun will promote flowering and apple production.

• **WATERING**
Water your apple tree regularly, especially in the first two years following planting. It is also possible to keep it in a pot on a terrace or balcony; it will then be necessary to water it regularly during the growing season (March through September).

• **POTTING**
Every 3 years in the spring, in a larger pot of 1 - 1 ½ inches. Use potting soil, making sure to put a bed of clay pellets at the bottom of the pot to facilitate drainage.

1. Collect about ten pips to maximize your chances of success. Rinse them with water to clean the flesh of the apple and prevent rot.

2. Place the seeds between paper towels or cotton balls moistened with lukewarm water and place them in a small container. Put them in the refrigerator for about four weeks, they need cold to germinate. In nature, winter takes care of this step. Be sure to keep the substrate moist during this time.

3. Prepare a pot with holes, 4 inches (10 cm) in diameter, with clay pebbles at the bottom and seedling soil. You can use tweezers to transfer the sprouted seed from the cotton to the jar. Bury it lightly, then place the pot in the sun and keep the soil moist.

4. After six to eight weeks, your apple tree will reach about 12 inches (30 cm) in height. You can then plant it in the ground but wait until fall to do so.

It will take about ten years for your little apple tree to produce its first fruits. You should know before participating in this long-term project that apples don't breed true from their seeds, so your tree should be considered ornamental as it is not likely to produce very desirable fruits.

Daucus carota

Carrot

YOU CAN'T GROW A NEW CARROT FROM CUTTINGS, BUT YOU CAN GROW THEIR LEAFY GREEN TOP. HOWEVER, IF YOU LET THE TOPS BLOOM, YOU CAN COLLECT THE SEEDS AND SOW THEM.

Family: Apiaceae
Origin: Afghanistan
Best time to propagate: spring, summer
GROW CUTTINGS IN WATER AND HARVEST THE GREENS

Plant care

- **PLANTING SEEDS**
From March to July.
- **WATERING**
Regular light watering, keeping the soil evenly moist. Take care to increase in the case of drought.

1. Cut the head of a carrot 2 inches (5 cm) from the top.

2. Put it to soak in water with the flesh submerged. Place it in the light in a room between 65°F–68°F (18°C–20°C).

3. A few days later, the tops will begin to regrow.

4. As soon as they measure 4 to 6 inches (10 to 15 cm), you can cut and cook them!

Producing carrot seeds

1. When the tops have grown about 4 inches (10 cm), plant the carrot in the garden directly in the ground and in the sun. Don't bury the orange carrot flesh too deeply.

2. Water regularly to keep the soil moist.

3. The roots will develop, and the tops will continue to grow until they flower. You can then collect the seeds and plant them to obtain carrots!

Sweet potato

Ipomoea batatas

PROPAGATING SWEET POTATOES FROM CUTTINGS IS EASY, BUT YOU REALLY NEED A GARDEN BED TO GROW THEM PROPERLY. IT'S WORTH TRYING IF YOU HAVE THE SPACE THOUGH AS IT IS A PRETTY PLANT AND A KEY INGREDIENT FOR SOME REALLY EXCELLENT SOUPS!

Family: Convolvulaceae
Origin: South America
Best time to take a cutting: the end of winter
PROPAGATE IN WATER

1 Stick three toothpicks into a sweet potato to hold it over a glass of water with the bottom half submerged. Place this cutting in a bright room, out of direct sunlight, at around 68°F (20°C). Change the water once a week. Wait a few weeks before you see the roots develop and the first stems sprout.

2 Once the stems have developed 5 to 6 leaves and are at least 4 inches (10 cm) tall, you can cut them. For 4-inch stems, cut flush with the potato, for longer stems, cut after the first leaf.

3 Place these branches, in turn, in a vase half-filled with water. Place them near a window, in a heated room between 65°F–68°F (18°C–20°C). Watch the water level and add more regularly.

4 About ten days later, small white roots will develop. It will then be time to plant your cuttings! Use a pot about 4 inches (10 cm) in diameter. Fill it with seedling soil. Make a hole in the potting soil and gently slip the cutting into it, without damaging the roots, then cover by packing lightly.

5 Water regularly to keep the soil moist and watch for signs of development: new leaves and elongation of the stem.

You can harvest in September when the foliage begins to turn yellow.

SAME TECHNIQUE *Potatoes*

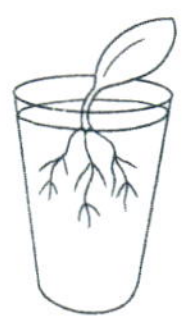

Plant care

- **CULTIVATION**
In the spring, from April to May, it is time to plant your cuttings in the vegetable garden. In preparation, make small mounds and plant them 12 inches (30 cm) apart, in rows approximately 3 ft (1 m) apart.
- **EXPOSURE**
Full sun.
- **WATERING**
Water very well just after planting, then regularly so as to keep the soil moist as the sweet potato doesn't fare well in drought.

Allium porrum

Leek

DON'T THROW AWAY YOUR LEEK LEFTOVERS, THEY ARE ONE OF THOSE VEGETABLES THAT MAKE PERFECT "INFINITE" CUTTINGS!

Family: Liliaceae
Origin: Middle East
Best time to take a cutting: year-round
A CUTTING WILL TAKE ROOT IN WATER

Plant care

You can leave the leek in water for as long as you want. After about three weeks, you will have a whole leek, ready to be cooked. You can then cut the stem 2 inches (5 cm) from the roots, put it back in water and thus regenerate a leek indefinitely!

1. Cut the stem about 1 inch (5 cm) from its roots. Soak the roots in a container filled with water at room temperature.

2. Place the cutting in the light in a room with a temperature of 65°F–68°F (18°C–20°C).

3. Change the water every two days or so, so that the roots do not rot.

4. After three to four days, you will see the stem lengthen and one week later the green leaves develop. You can then cut them according to your desires to cook them!

Lettuce

Lactuca sativa

GROW YOUR SALAD WITH ITS FEET IN WATER!

Family: Asteraceae
Origin: Middle East
Best time to take a cutting: year-round
Germinate in water, from a lettuce base

Plant care

No special maintenance, apart from the advice mentioned here.

1. Cut the base of a head of lettuce. Soak it in a container filled with water at room temperature. Place it in a light in a room with a temperature of 65°F–68°F (18°C–20°C).

2. Change the water about every two days to prevent the roots from rotting.

3. After four to five days, you will see its new leaves grow! It will take about three weeks to have a new thick salad that you can taste!

4. Cross-check the base and start again, the multiplication is infinite!

This technique works particularly well if you are able to buy hydroponically grown heads of lettuce that are sold with their roots still attached.

CHAPTER 3

Decorative plants

Foliage

Flowering

Succulents

Ficus elastica

Rubber

SAME TECHNIQUE
Aeschynanthus,
Fiddle-leaf fig,
Climbing philodendron

IF YOU DREAM OF AN INDOOR TREE, GO FOR RUBBER: IT CAN REACH UP TO 16 FT HIGH.

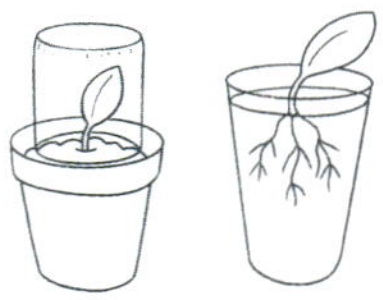

Family: Moraceae
Origin: India
Best time to take a cutting: spring, summer
TAKES ROOT IN SMOTHERED SOIL, OR IN WATER, FROM A STEM

Plant care

- **EXPOSURE**
Adapts everywhere, in partial shade and in a bright area, but without direct sun.
- **WATERING**
– In spring and summer, twice a week, the soil must dry out on the surface by ¾ to 1 inches (2 to 3 cm). Spray its foliage every 2 or 3 days.
– In winter, water approximately once a week.
- **POTTING**
In the spring, every two years, in a compost for house plants as long as the plant allows it. When its size is too large for repotting, proceed to a surfacing by replacing the top soil only.

Moist soil cutting

1. Take a stem about 4 to 6 inches (10 to 15 cm) long, cutting at an angle and just below a node. Remove the leaves to keep only three or four at the top of the stem.

2. Then place it in a pot filled with seedling soil, pushing it down a few centimeters. Water well to moisten the soil.

3. Place the pot under a glass bell jar or under transparent plastic to recreate a greenhouse effect that will maintain a good level of humidity and thus promote the taking of the cutting.

4. Place the pot in a bright and warm place, at a temperature of 68°F–75°F (20°C–24°C), and water as soon as the soil dries on the surface.

5. As soon as the first roots appear, after a month, a month and a half, remove the bell or plastic.

Rooting cuttings in water

1. Take a stem about 4 to 6 inches (10 to 15 cm) long, cutting at an angle and just below a node. Remove the leaves to keep only three or four at the top of the stem.

2. Place it in a glass container filled, ideally, with fresh water (this will allow you to change the water less often). With tap water, change it regularly, at least once a week. If you place a piece of charcoal in the bottom of the container the water will stay clean longer.

GOOD TO KNOW

If you want to propagate a leaf, it is possible, just make sure to take a petiole with a leaf. Even though this petiole is small, it's where the dormant buds reside, enabling a leaf to give birth to an entirely new plant.

3 Find a bright location, out of direct sunlight, avoid drafts and sources of heat that are too close (radiators, fireplaces). Its environment must be humid and warm, around 66°F (19°C).

4 Watch for the appearance of the first roots, then transfer your cutting to a pot as soon as they have grown about an inch (3 cm).

5 Use a pot about 4 inches (10 cm) in diameter. Fill it with potting soil: a light, fine and draining potting soil. This type of soil is ideal for promoting the rooting of the cutting. Make a hole in the soil to gently slip the cutting into it, without damaging the roots. Then, cover by packing lightly.

6 Water regularly to keep the soil moist and watch for signs of development: new leaves and elongation of the stem.

Monstera

Monstera deliciosa

MONSTROUSLY DELICIOUS! ITS LEAVES ARE NOT PERFORATED TO SCARE, BUT TO LET THE LIGHT THROUGH AND ENLIVEN THE FOLIAGE.

Family: Araceae
Origin: tropical rainforests of Central and South America
Best time to take a cutting: year-round, but preferable in spring or summer, while the plant is growing.
Takes root in water from a shoot, or by layering

Plant care

• **EXPOSURE**
Bright, without direct sunlight, avoiding drafts.

• **WATERING / FERTILIZING**
Water regularly to keep the soil moist. Wait for the soil to dry on the surface between two waterings.
– From March to October, amend with liquid house plant food every three weeks.
– Once your plant has grown well, mist the foliage regularly year-round, with non-calcareous water (except the new leaves). To maintain ambient humidity, place a bed of wet clay pellets or gravel in a saucer, on which you will place the pot.

• **POTTING**
In the spring, every two years, in a potting soil mix as long as the plant allows it. When its size is too large for repotting, proceed to a top-dressing method by replacing the surface soil only.

SAME TECHNIQUE
Pothos

Separating the offset

This technique is recommended only if your mother plant has a nice form, otherwise it would be a shame to strip it.

1 To improve your chances of taking, choose a shoot of about 2 inches (5 cm), with at least three leaves. Dig it up carefully and use a clean knife or pruner to cut it with a piece of root. Don't forget to plug the hole!

2 Place the cutting in a container filled with water at room temperature, making sure to immerse the roots well, keeping the leaves out of the water.

3 Then place your cutting in the light, but away from direct sunlight which could both damage its leaves and the roots that will develop. Also avoid drafts.

4 After a couple weeks, the first white roots will begin to develop. Once they have reached 1½ to 2 inches (4 to 5 cm) in length, it will be time to plant it in the ground.

Layering

This technique is ideal if your plant becomes a bit too big and you'd like to thin it out.

1 You will have to identify a portion of stem that you are going to bury. Here, there is no question of cutting the stem. Or at least not yet! This stem must be flexible and healthy and include at least one aerial root.

2 Bury it in such a way as to push this aerial root into the ground and secure it with small pins so that it does not move.

3 Water regularly to keep the soil moist.

4 After four weeks, its tap roots will have developed, and it will then be time to cut the stem to separate it from the parent plant.

Hedera helix

Ivy

IVY IS A CREEPING, CLIMBING PLANT. IF YOU'RE LOOKING FOR QUICK FOLIAGE, THEN THIS PLANT IS A GOOD CHOICE. IVY IS EASY TO MAINTAIN, INDOORS AND OUT.

Family: Araliacea
Origin: Europe and Asia
Best time to take a cutting: year-round
TAKES ROOT IN WATER FROM A STEM, OR BY LAYERING

Plant care

- **EXPOSURE**
Bright indirect light or partly shaded.
- **WATERING**
In a pot, the soil dries out much more quickly, so be sure to keep the soil moist.
– In spring and summer, water regularly 2 to 3 times a week depending on the heat.
– In winter, let nature take its course! But if it does not rain for several weeks, water a little.
- **POTTING**
The ivy develops rapidly, so repotting every year in the spring is necessary.

Rooting cuttings in water

1. Cut three stems at least 4 to 6 inches (10 to 15 cm) long. Remove the basal leaves to keep only the three or four at the end. Put them in a vase filled with water, making sure to keep the leaves out of the water.

2. As soon as the roots appear, after about two weeks, plant them in a pot filled with seedling soil. Planting them by three allows you to have a more substantial plant!

3. Place your cuttings in a bright place, without direct sun, and in a heated room between 65°F–70°F (18°C–21°C). Water regularly to keep the soil moist.

Layering

This technique is ideal if you want to flesh out your ivy.

1. Select a healthy, vigorous stem that has multiple nodes. Bend it without breaking it towards a pot filled with potting soil that you will place right next to the mother plant.

2. Push the nodes into the ground, holding the stem to the ground with small pins to prevent it from moving. Water to keep the soil moist.

3. After three to six months, the stem takes root. You can then separate it from the parent plant.

Tradescantia

Spiderwort

SAME TECHNIQUE
Aeschynanthe

IF YOU THINK YOU HAVE A BROWN THUMB, THIS "WANDERING DUDE" WILL PROVE YOU WRONG AND RESTORE YOUR CONFIDENCE.

Family: Commelinaceae
Origin: North and South America
Best time to take a cutting: spring, summer
TAKES ROOT IN WATER OR SOIL, FROM A STEM

Plant care

- **EXPOSURE**
Bright light stimulates the pretty coloring of the foliage, but do not expose it to direct sunlight and keep it away from drafts.
- **WATERING**
Neither too much water nor too little.
– In spring and summer, watering 2 to 3 times a week depending on the heat.
– In winter, about once or twice a week. Wait until the soil dries on the surface by ¾ to 1 inch (2 to 3 cm) before watering again.
- **POTTING**
Every two years, when the plant is too cramped.

Rooting cuttings in water

1. Take a stem cutting 2 to 3 inches (5 to 8 cm) long. Remove all leaves except the top three or four.

2. Immerse the stem in water, making sure to keep its top out of the water.

3. As soon as the first roots are an inch long (3 cm), it is time to put your cutting in a pot.

4. Use a pot about 4 inches (10 cm) in diameter. Fill it with seedling soil: a light, fine and draining soil. This type of soil is ideal for promoting the rooting of the cutting.

5. Make a hole in the soil to gently slip the cutting into it, without damaging the roots, then cover by packing lightly.

6. Water regularly to keep the soil moist and watch for signs of development: new leaves and elongation of the stem.

Moist soil cutting

1. Take a stem 2 to 3 inches (5 to 8 cm) long. Remove the leaves to leave only three or four at the end.
2. Prepare a pot 3 inches (6 cm) in diameter, fill the bottom with clay pebbles and seedling soil. Make a hole and plant the cutting. Pack the soil well around the stem.
3. Water well to moisten the soil. Place a glass or plastic cloche to create the effect of a small greenhouse.
4. Place the pot in a bright and warm place (between 68°F–75°F / 20–24°C) and water as soon as the soil dries on the surface.
5. As soon as the first roots appear after 4 to 6 weeks, remove the bell.

Elephant ear

Alocasia polly

SAME TECHNIQUE
Bird of paradise, taro

THIS PLANT WITH LARGE RIBBED LEAVES EVOKES AN ELEPHANT'S EAR - IT ALSO PRODUCES MANY "PUPS". ITS APPEARANCE IS AS MAJESTIC AS IT IS UNIQUE AND IS HIGHLY DECORATIVE.

Plant care

- **EXPOSURE**
Bright, without direct sunlight, 65°F–70°F (18°C–22°C).
- **WATERING**
Mist foliage every day with freshwater.
– In spring and in summer, water regularly, twice a week, letting the substrate dry out on the surface between two waterings.
– In winter, water less often, let the substrate dry out to the depth of 1 inch (3 cm) before watering again. Keep away from heat sources that dry out foliage.
- **NUTRIENTS**
Use liquid fertilizer for house plants every two weeks, from the end of March to the end of September.
- **POTTING**
Every 2 to 3 years, in the spring, between March and May.

Family: Araceae
Origin: tropical forests of Asia
Best time to take a cutting: spring, summer, the heat ensures a better grip of the cuttings.
STEMS FROM A SPROUT

1 Unpot the plant, or directly and delicately remove the soil surrounding the shoots by hand. These generally develop at the foot of the mother plant.

2 Take them, keeping a rhizome well, so as to keep roots. This will increase the chances of recovery. Eliminate the basal leaves to keep only the young leaves.

3 Prepare pots adapted to the size of your offset. Line them at the bottom with clay pebbles, then pour in seedling soil. Make a hole and plant the sprout, packing the soil well all around.

4 Water in such a way as to keep the soil always a little moist and place your cutting in a bright room heated to 68°F (20°C).

5 As soon as you see a new leaf springing up, it's a sign that the cutting has taken!

Money tree

Pachira aquatica

THIS PARASOL-LIKE PLANT NEEDS LITTLE MAINTENANCE. IN EFFECT, IT STORES WATER IN ITS TRUNK, WHICH ENABLES IT TO BE WATERED LESS FREQUENTLY.

Family: Bombacaceae
Origin: marshy areas of Asia, Central and South America
Best time to take a cutting: September
Takes root in water or soil, from a stem

Plant care

- **EXPOSURE**
Bright, indirect light
- **WATERING**
Its soil should be kept cool, but not too wet. Set the pot on a saucer filled with wet clay pebbles. Evaporation will maintain a good ambient humidity.
– Use liquid fertilizer for house plants, every two weeks, from the end of March to the end of September. Water it as soon as the soil dries on the surface.
– In winter, reduce watering to once a week.
- **POTTING**
Every year in the spring in a slightly larger pot.

Rooting cuttings in water

1. Take the head of the stem with a length of about 4 inches (10 cm). Remove all the leaves to keep only two at the end. Dip the stem in water, making sure to keep the leaves out of the water.

2. As soon as the first roots grow to an inch (3 cm), it is time to put it in a pot.

3. Use a pot about 4 inches (10 cm) in diameter. Fill it with seedling soil. Make a hole in the soil to gently slip the cutting into it, without damaging the roots, then cover by packing lightly.

4. Water regularly to keep the soil moist and watch for signs of development: new leaves and elongation of the stem.

5. After three to four weeks, roots should have developed. It will then be time to repot your cutting in a slightly larger pot with soil for house plants.

Moist soil cutting

1. Take the head of the stem over a length of about 4 inches (10 cm). Remove all the leaves to keep only two at the end.

2. In a pot filled with seedling soil, make a small hole, and plant the cutting. Pack the soil well around the stem. Water well to moisten the soil.

3. Place a glass bell to ensure the effects of a small greenhouse. Then place the pot in a bright and warm place (between 65–68°F/20–24°C) and water as soon as the soil dries on the surface.

4. Aerate approximately every two days by lifting the bell.

5. After three to four weeks, roots should have developed. It will then be time to repot your cutting in a slightly larger pot with soil for house plants.

Syngonium podophyllum

Syngoniu

FROM THE SAME FAMILY AS THE PHILODENDRONS, THE SYNGONIUM HAS THE CHARACTERISTIC OF PRODUCING STEM ROOTS THAT SPREAD VERY QUICKLY.

Family: Araceae
Origin: Central and South America, Africa, and Australia
Best time to take a cutting: March and April
TAKES ROOT IN SOIL, FROM A STEM

Moist soil cutting

1 Take, at the foot of the mother plant, a young shoot that has small aerial roots. Cut it under a node (this is where the new earth roots will grow). Remove the lower leaves.

2 Prepare a pot about 3 inches (6 cm) in diameter, fill the bottom with clay pebbles and add seedling soil. Make a small hole and plant the cutting, making sure to bury the aerial roots very lightly. Place the pot on a saucer. Firmly tamp the soil to keep the stem straight.

3 Water directly into the saucer, with a full glass of water. The soil will thus drink from below, this avoids soaking the soil.

4 To accelerate the development of the roots, place a glass or plastic bell to create the effect of a small greenhouse. Place the pot in a bright place, without direct sunlight, and warm (68°F/20°C). Keep the soil moist by watering through the saucer.

5 After two to three weeks, new leaves should develop. At this time, remove the bell.

Plant care

- **EXPOSURE**
Bright, indirect sunlight, in a room heated to 68°F (20°C).
- **WATERING**
The soil should be kept cool, but not too wet.
– Place the pot on a saucer filled with wet clay pebbles. Evaporation will maintain a good ambient humidity. Mist its foliage once or twice a week with fresh water.
– In winter, water a little less often leaving the soil to dry on the surface for the top inch (2 to 3 cm).
- **NUTRIENTS**
Feed liquid fertilizer for house plants, every two weeks from the end of March to the end of September.
- **POTTING**
In the spring, every three years in a slightly larger pot. Place clay pebbles at the bottom to facilitate drainage, then potting soil for house plants.

Peperomia

Peperomia

THE PEPEROMIAS HAVE FOLIAGE WITH A RANGE OF TEXTURES AND PATTERNS. THERE ARE A MULTITUDE OF VARIETIES THAT ARE ALL PROPAGATED THE SAME WAY.

Family: Piperaceae
Origin: Antilles, South America
Best time to take a cutting: early spring
TAKES ROOT IN SOIL, SMOTHERED, AND IN WATER, FROM A LEAF

Plant care

• **EXPOSURE**
Bright, but without direct sun which would burn its foliage. Install it near a window, in a heated room between 50°F–68°F (10°C–20°C).

• **WATERING**
Watch out for excess! Let the topsoil dry thoroughly (1 inch/3 cm) between two waterings.
– In spring, water once a week.
– In summer, when the heat is stronger, water up to two times a week.
– In winter, reduce the water supply. If the air is dry, set the pot on a saucer filled with wet clay pebbles.

• **POTTING**
In the spring, as soon as the roots come out from the jar. Place clay pellets in the bottom to help with drainage, then potting soil.

Rooting cuttings in water

1 Tear off a healthy leaf and cut the petiole about 1 inch (3 cm) from the base of the leaf (see page 27).

2 Dip this little rod in the water, making sure to keep its head above water. Place a piece of charcoal in the bottom of the glass to keep the water clean longer. Readjust the water level so that the stem is still swimming.

3 As soon as the first roots are an inch long (3 cm), it is time to put it in a pot. Use a pot about 4 inches (10 cm) in diameter. Fill it with seedling soil, light, fine and draining, ideal for promoting rooting. Make a hole in the soil to gently slip the cutting into it, without damaging the roots, then cover by packing lightly.

4 Water regularly to keep the soil moist and watch for signs of development: new leaves and elongation of the stem.

Moist soil cutting

1 Tear off a healthy leaf and cut the petiole about an inch (3 cm) from the base of the leaf. Lay the sheet on its back, on a clean surface (e.g., wooden board). Cut perpendicularly, over a maximum of half an inch (1 cm), using a fine blade, the veins which are on the back of the sheet (see page 27).

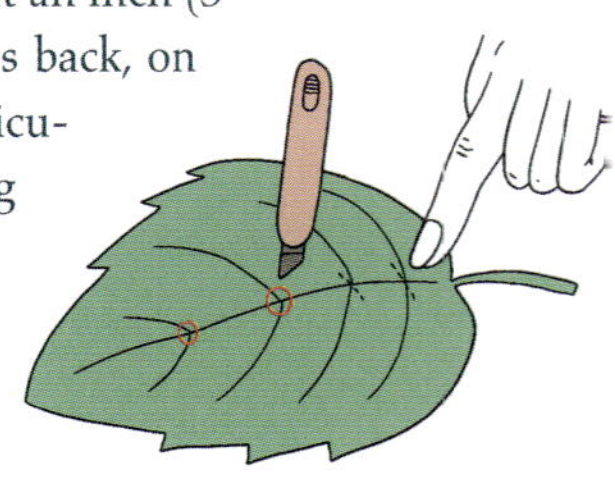

TIPS

- Use several leaves at once to increase your odds of success.
- Be sure to choose a healthy leaf so that you limit the risk of rot, or disease.

2 In a pierced terracotta pot, place clay balls at the bottom, then seedling soil. Make a small hole in the ground, in which you can push the petiole while laying the leaf on the soil with the notch on the ground side. To keep the sheet flat against the ground, place small pebbles on its edges.

3 Water regularly, by basting the pot (by dipping it in a basin) for fifteen minutes every ten days, so as to keep the soil slightly moist without wetting the leaf. Cover the pot with a bell, glass or plastic, or even with a transparent plastic film. Place it in a warm room 68°F–75°F (20°C–24°C), bright, but without direct sunlight.

4 Seedlings should appear between three and six weeks later depending on the plant. Wait until the root system is well developed for the repot.

Chinese money plant

Pilea peperomioides

SAME TECHNIQUE

Tiger grass

THIS PLANT PRODUCES A LOT OF OFFSETS, A VERY FREQUENT PHENOMENON WHEN A CUTTING, CREATED IN WATER, IS POTTED IN SOIL. ALL "OFFSETS" ARE NOT SUITABLE FOR CUTTINGS. IT IS ESSENTIAL THAT YOUR SAMPLES ARE HEALTHY AND MATURE; DON'T TAKE YOUNG SPROUTS.

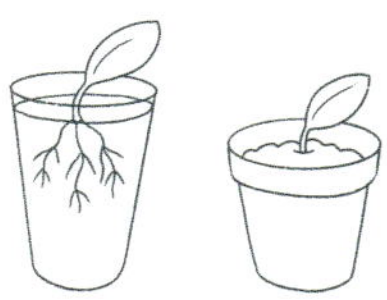

Family: Urticaceae
Origin: China
Best time to take a cutting: year-round, but the best time is in spring, when the plant is growing and producing suckers.
Takes root in water or soil, from a shoot

Plant care

- **EXPOSURE**
Strong indirect light.
- **WATERING**
Regular.
– In winter, once or twice a week.
– In summer, 2 to 3 times a week. be careful not to let the water stagnate. To do this, put clay pellets at the bottom of the pot to drain the water.
- **POTTING**
Every two years, in the spring, when the roots come out of the pot.

Rooting cuttings in water

1. Spot an offset from your plant. There may be several! The one you choose should be at least 2 inches (5 cm) tall and have three to four leaves. Scrape the soil to detach these small shoots with delicacy, cutting them so as to recover as many roots as possible. Be sure to use a clean, sharp tool so as not to damage the cutting or the mother plant.

2. If you have managed to keep good roots, then you can repot them directly. Otherwise, you can place these shoots in water at room temperature, making sure to immerse the roots well, keeping the leaves out of the water.

3. Then place your cutting away from drafts and direct sunlight, which could damage both its leaves and the roots that develop. Then wait...

4. After two to three weeks, new roots will appear and the cutting can be replanted in light, well-drained soil suitable for your plant.

GOOD TO KNOW

The leaves of this plant are attracted to the sun, so do not hesitate to turn it from time to time so that it develops a balanced form.

Rooting cuttings in soil

1 The first step is the same as for the preparation of the cutting in water.

2 Once the offset has been collected, prepare a pot 2 ½ inches (6 cm) in diameter by covering the bottom with clay pebbles and fill it with seedling soil. Make a small hole in it with a pencil and place your cutting in it. Pack the soil to keep the stem straight. Water generously.

Hypoestes

Polka dot plant

SAME TECHNIQUE
Mosaic plant

ITS VERY DECORATIVE FOLIAGE, SPOTTED WITH CREAM-WHITE, PINK OR RED, HAS GIVEN IT ITS NAME: THE EPHELIDES PLANT, THAT IS TO SAY, "WITH FRECKLES." IT IS VERY DECORATIVE AND IS EASILY CUT.

Family: Acanthaceae
Origin: Madagascar
Best time to take a cutting: spring, summer
Takes root in water or soil, from a stem

Plant care

- **EXPOSURE**

Little light, especially no direct sun. Also keep it away from drafts.

- **WATERING**

Neither too much water nor too little. Its soil must remain moist:
– In spring and summer, watering every 2 to 3 days.
– In winter, about twice a week. Place the pot on a saucer filled with wet clay pebbles. Evaporation will humidify the surrounding air. Mist its foliage daily with fresh water. It is ideal in a terrarium (confined environment with glass walls).

- **POTTING**

In the spring, every three years, with potting soil.
Place clay pebbles at the bottom of the pot to aid drainage.

Rooting cuttings in water

1. Take a stem 2 or 3 inches (5 to 8 cm) long. Remove the leaves, leaving only three or four at the end.

2. Immerse the stem in water, being careful to keep the leaves out of the water.

3. As soon as the first roots appear an inch long (2 to 3 cm), it is time to put it in a pot.

4. Use a pot about 4 inches (10 cm) in diameter. Fill it with seedling soil: a light, fine and draining soil. This type of soil is ideal for promoting the rooting of the cutting. Make a hole in the soil to gently slip the cutting into it, without damaging the roots, then cover by packing lightly.

5. Water regularly to keep the soil moist and watch for signs of development: new leaves and elongation of the stem.

Moist soil cutting

1. Take a stem 2 to 3 inches (5 to 8 cm) long. Remove the leaves to leave only three or four at the end.

2. In a pot filled with seedling soil, make a small hole, and plant the cutting. Pack the soil well around the stem.

3. Water well to moisten the soil. Place a glass or plastic bell to ensure the effects of a small greenhouse.

4. Place the pot in a bright and warm place (68°F–75°F / 20°C–24°C) and water as soon as the soil dries on the surface.

5. Aerate approximately every two days by lifting the bell. As soon as the first roots appear, after a month, a month and a half, remove the bell.

Maranta leucoreuna

Prayer plant

KNOWN FOR ITS EXTRAORDINARY FOLIAGE, THIS PLANT GETS ITS NAME FROM ITS TENDENCY TO CURL UP FOR THE NIGHT—AN EXAMPLE OF A DIURNAL RHYTHM.

Plant care

• **EXPOSURE**
In subdued light because the direct sun dulls its foliage; also keep it away from drafts.

• **WATERING**
– In spring and summer, water twice a week and mist it every day.
– In winter, water once a week and mist 2 to 3 times a week. Set the pot on a saucer filled with wet clay pebbles. Evaporation will thus humidify the ambient air.
– To revive the flamboyant colors of the maranta, place a piece of charcoal in the earth.

• **POTTING**
Every year in the spring, in a soil for potted plants mixed half with peat moss or other acidic mix, with a bed of clay pellets at the bottom.

Family: Marantaceae
Origin: Latin America, The Antilles
Best time to take a cutting: spring
TAKES ROOT IN WATER

1 Take, by cutting at an angle and just below a node, a stem about 4 to 6 inches (10 to 15 cm) long. Remove the leaves to keep only three at the top of the stem.

2 Place it in a glass container filled, ideally, with fresh water. With tap water, change it regularly, at least once a week. Place a piece of charcoal in the bottom of the container, the water will stay clean longer and this will promote root development.

3 Place the pot under a glass or plastic bell jar to recreate a greenhouse effect that will maintain a good level of humidity and promote the development of the cutting. Place the pot in a bright place, without direct sunlight, and warm 65°F–70°F (18°C–22°C).

4 Watch for the appearance of the first roots. As soon as these have grown an inch to an inch and a half (3 to 4 cm), remove the bell. It is time to plant it in a pot!

5 Use a pot about 5 inches (12 cm) in diameter. Not taller, as the foliage grows more than the roots. Place clay pellets in the bottom and fill it with seedling soil: a light, fine and draining soil. Moisten the soil by watering generously. Make a hole in the soil to gently slip the cutting into it, without damaging the roots, then cover by packing lightly.

6 Water regularly to keep the soil moist and watch for signs of development: new leaves and elongation of the stem.

Zebra plant

Aphelandra squarrosa

THE ZEBRA PLANT IS AMAZING WITH ITS GREEN AND WHITE-RIBBED FOLIAGE. ITS BRIGHT YELLOW FLOWERS ARE IS JUST AS IMPRESSIVE!

Plant care

• EXPOSURE
Strong, indirect light

• WATERING / PRUNING
Its soil should be kept cool, but not too wet. Set the pot on a saucer filled with wet clay pebbles. Evaporation will help maintain a good level of ambient humidity. Mist its foliage once or twice a week with fresh water.
– In the spring, prune the first pair of leaves. This will allow the plant to renew its foliage so you can make cuttings. Remove its flower when it begins to fade.
– In winter, install in a cool room (59°F/15°C), stop adding fertilizer and reduce watering.

• NUTRIENTS
Liquid fertilizer for house plants, every two weeks, from March to October.

• POTTING
In the spring, every three years.

Family: Acanthaceae
Origin: South America
Best time to take a cutting: spring, summer
TAKES ROOT IN SOIL, FROM A STEM

1 Take the head of the stem with a length of 2 to 4 inches (5 to 8 cm). Remove all the leaves, keeping the petioles (small stem that connects the leaf to the mother stem) to keep only one leaf at the end.

2 In a pot about 4 inches (10 cm) in diameter, filled with seedling soil, make a small hole, and plant the cutting. Pack the soil well around the stem. Water well to moisten the soil. Place a glass or plastic bell to create a greenhouse effect.

3 Place the pot in a bright and warm place (68°F–75°F / 20°C–24°C) and water as soon as the soil dries on the surface.

4 Ventilate approximately every two days by removing the bell for about fifteen minutes.

5 Wait six to eight weeks to see a new leaf appear, a sign that the cutting has taken.

Begonia rex

Begonia

MANY BEGONIAS ARE APPRECIATED FOR THEIR FLOWERS. THIS ONE HAS AMAZING FOLIAGE! PINK, GREY, GREEN, RED, SILVER, ITS REFLECTIONS OFFER AN INCREDIBLE AND FASCINATING COLOR PALETTE.

Family: Begoniaceae
Origin: Asia
Best time to take a cutting: beginning of spring
TAKES ROOT IN WATER OR SOIL, FROM A LEAF

Plant care

• **EXPOSURE**
Bright, but without direct sun, which would burn its foliage. Install it near a window in a heated room between 50°F–68°F (10°C–20°C).

• **WATERING**
Watch out for excess! Let the soil dry out well on the surface (about 1 inch/3 cm) between two waterings.
– Water once a week in spring.
– In summer, when the heat is stronger, water up to two times a week.
– In winter, you can reduce the water intake. If the air is too dry, set the pot on a saucer filled with wet clay pebbles. Evaporation humidifies the surrounding air.

• **POTTING**
Every three years, in the spring.

Rooting cuttings in water

1 Take healthy leaves and cut the petiole about 1 inch (3 cm) from the base of each leaf.

2 Dip the stems in water, making sure to keep the leaves out of the water. Place a piece of charcoal in the bottom of the glass to keep the water clean longer. Readjust the water level regularly so that the stems are constantly bathing.

3 As soon as the first roots measure 1 to 1½ inches (3 or 4 cm), it is time to put them each in a pot. Use pots about 4 inches (10 cm) in diameter. Fill them with seedling soil—light, fine and well-draining—ideal for encouraging rooting. Make a hole in the soil to gently slide the cuttings into it, without damaging the roots. Then, cover by packing lightly.

4 Water regularly to keep the soil moist and watch for signs of development: new leaves and elongation of the stem.

▸▸▸

Cut the petiole to about an inch.

Immerse the petiole in water,
making sure the leaf remains dry.

Cut the leaf veins.

Put the petioles in the soil.

Lay small pebbles on the leaves to ensure contact with the soil.

Put the pot under a cloche.

Rooting cuttings in soil

1. Take healthy leaves and cut their petiole about 1 inch (3 cm) from the base of the leaf.

2. Lay the leaves upside down on a clean surface. Using a sharp, thin blade, cut the veins on the back of the leaf with perpendicular incisions no more than half an inch (1 cm) long.

3. Prepare a pot with seedling soil, press the petiole into the soil and lay the leaf on the moist soil with the notch on the ground side. To keep the sheet flat, place small pebbles around its edges. Cover the container and the cutting under a glass or plastic cover or under a transparent film.

4. Place your pot in a warm room around 68°F–75°F (20°C–24°C), bright, but without direct sunlight. Water regularly, basting in such a way as to keep the soil slightly moist without wetting the leaves.

5. Seedlings should appear between three and six weeks depending on the plant. Wait until the root system is well developed to repot them.

TIPS

- *Avoid wetting the leaves when watering, it is best to drench from below, using a saucer.*
- *Propagate several leaves to have more chances of success.*
- *Be sure to choose a healthy leaf, as there is a high risk of rot.*

Hoya

Hoya

THIS PLANT OFFERS A SURPRISING FLOWER THAT LOOKS LIKE PORCELAIN. WITH SPECIAL CARE SOME VARIETIES CAN FLOWER YEAR-ROUND.

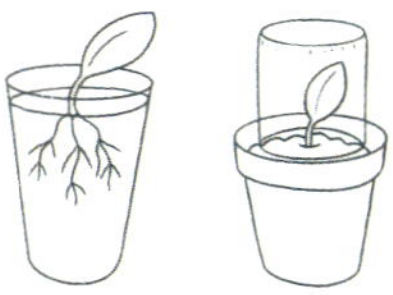

Family: Aclepiadoiceae
Origin: Asia, Australia, and the Pacific Islands
Best time to take a cutting: spring, summer
Takes root in water or soil, from a stem

Plant care

- **EXPOSURE**

Bright, indirect light

- **WATERING**

– In spring and summer, water about once a week.
– In winter, water a little less, once every 15 days. Empty the saucer well after watering so that water does not stagnate at the bottom. You can also soak the pot for thirty minutes. This avoids wetting the foliage of the hoya.

- **POTTING**

In the spring, every two years in a slightly larger pot. Place clay pellets at the bottom of the pot to aid drainage, then potting soil for flowering plants.

Rooting cuttings in water

1. Cut a stem 4 inches (10 cm) long. Remove most of the leaves, with only two or three remaining at the end. Immerse the stem in water, making sure to keep its leaves out of the water.

2. As soon as the first roots appear a few centimeters, it is time to put it in the ground. Use a pot about 4 inches (10 cm) in diameter. Fill it with seedling soil: a light, fine and draining soil. Make a hole in the soil to gently slip the cutting into it, without damaging the roots, then cover by packing lightly.

3. Place the cutting in a bright room, without direct sunlight, and heated between 68°F–75°F (20–24°C).

4. Water regularly to keep the soil moist and watch for signs of development: new leaves and elongation of the stem.

Moist soil cutting

1. As with the cutting in water, the preparation of the cutting consists of taking a stem 4 inches (10 cm) long. Remove most of the leaves, with only two or three remaining at the end.

2. In a pot filled with seedling soil, make a small hole and plant the cutting. Pack the soil well around the stem. Water well to moisten the soil. Place a glass or plastic bell to create a greenhouse effect.

3. Place the pot in a bright place, without direct sunlight, and warm (between 68°F–75°F / 20°C–24°C) and water as soon as the soil dries on the surface. Aerate approximately every two days by lifting the bell.

4. As soon as the first roots appear, after about a month, remove the bell.

Pink jasmine

Jasminum polyanthum

JASMINE IS A CLIMBING PLANT WITH DARK GREEN FOLIAGE AND BEAUTIFUL WHITE FLOWERS. ITS SOFT AND INVITING FRAGRANCE WILL PERFUME THE WHOLE HOUSE!

Family: Oleaceae
Origin: China
Best time to take a cutting in water: April through September
Best time to root a cutting in soil: late summer, early fall
Best time to take a cutting by layering: spring
Can be taken in water or in the ground, from a stem, or by layering

Plant care

• **EXPOSURE**
Sunny (the sun promotes flowering) and away from the cold and drafts.

• **WATERING**
Water regularly to keep the soil moist. wait for the soil to dry on the surface between two waterings. To maintain ambient humidity, place a bed of damp gravel in a saucer, on which you will place the pot.

• **NUTRIENTS**
In summer, from March to October, add liquid flower plant fertilizer every two weeks.

• **POTTING**
In the spring, every two years, in a soil for flowering plants.

Rooting cuttings in water

1 Make several cuttings to increase your chances of success. Take young green stems 4 inches (10 cm) long. Cut them just below a node, this is where the roots will grow. Remove all the leaves to keep only three or four at the upper ends.

2 In a glass ideally filled with fresh water, place a piece of charcoal at the bottom to purify the water, and place your cuttings in the water, keeping their tops dry. Place them in a bright place, out of direct sunlight.

3 Add water regularly to maintain the same level. When the roots start to grow 1 inch (3 cm), after about two weeks, it's time to plant your cutting.

4 Prepare a pot about 4 inches (10 cm) in diameter, filled with seedling soil and place the cutting in the center. Water as soon as the soil dries slightly on the surface.

Rooting cuttings in soil

1 Cut a young 4-inch (10 cm) stem, in the same way as the cutting in water.

2 Prepare a pot 4 inches in diameter, filled with seedling soil, water, then make a small hole to plant the cutting. Pack the soil well around the stem.

3 Place the pot in a bright place, out of direct sunlight. Water as soon as the soil dries out slightly.

4 When new leaves appear, your cutting has taken root! It is then time to transplant it into a slightly larger pot with soil for flowering plants.

▶▶▶

Layering

1 Identify a portion of soft, healthy stem that you will bury. There is no question of cutting it yet!

2 Prepare a pot filled with seedling soil, then place it right next to the pot of the mother plant.

3 Lay your stem in this pot by blocking it in the ground with a pin or a simple pebble. The end of the rod must not be buried.

4 Keep the soil moist, because it is the part of the stem underground that will produce the roots.

5 After about three weeks, check that the roots have developed well by pulling lightly on the stem. If you feel a hook, it worked! You can then separate it from the mother plant.

Nerium oleander

Oleander

WHITE, PINK OR EVEN RED, OLEANDER OFFERS FLOWERS ALL SUMMER! PLANTED IN A GARDEN OR ON A TERRACE, IT IS VERY EASY TO TAKE CUTTINGS FROM IT.

Plant care

• **EXPOSURE**
Sunny. But shelter it all the same from the scorching summer sun.

• **WATERING / MAINTENANCE**
In a pot, the soil dries out much more quickly, be sure to keep it moist.
– In spring and summer, water regularly, 2 to 3 times a week depending on the temperature. Avoid wetting the leaves as this can encourage aphids and other pests.
– In winter, let nature take its course, but water a little if it does not rain for several weeks.

• **POTTING**
In the spring, every 2 or 3 years, in a well-drained pot.

TIPS

This plant is toxic, wash your hands well after handling!

Family: Apocynaceae
Origin: Mediterranean Basin
Best time to take a cutting: July and August
TAKES ROOT IN SOIL AND WATER, FROM A STEM

Rooting cuttings in soil

1 Cut stems without flowers 6 to 8 inches long (15 to 20 cm), they must be healthy. Make sure they don't show any signs of disease or pests. Cut under a node. Remove the basal leaves to keep only five or six at the end of the stems.

2 Prepare pots about 4 inches (10 cm) in diameter, fill with seedling soil, make a hole and plant your cuttings (only one per pot). Place them in a bright, heated room between 55°F–68°F (12°C–20°C).

3 Wait six weeks for roots to develop. You can then repot them in potting soil or plant them in the ground next spring.

Rooting cuttings in water

1 Take stems without flowers and prepare them in the same way as for the cutting in water. Immerse your cuttings in a glass container, keeping the leaves out of the water.

2 As soon as the roots appear, three to four weeks later, repot them in a pot about 4 inches (10 cm) in diameter, filled with seedling soil (only one per pot). Place them in a bright, heated room between 55°F–68°F (12°C–20°C).

3 Wait six weeks for roots to develop. You can then repot the cuttings in potting soil or plant them next spring.

Rosa

Rose

THERE ARE A MULTITUDE OF ROSES IN DIFFERENT SIZES, SHAPES AND COLORS; THERE IS SOMETHING FOR EVERY TASTE! ALL THEY ASK FOR IS SUN.

Family: Rosaceae
Origin: temperate and subtropical regions of the northern hemisphere
Best time to take a cutting: September
Takes root in the ground, from a stem (two possible techniques)

Plant care

• **EXPOSURE**
Sunny, but protect for burning mid-summer sun.

• **WATERING / MAINTENANCE**
In a pot, the soil dries out much more quickly, so be sure to keep the soil moist.
– In spring and summer, water regularly 2 to 3 times a week depending on the heat. Avoid wetting the leaves, which invites aphids and other parasites. Add some fertilizer to roses in the spring and don't forget to remove faded flowers to stimulate its growth and new flowering.
– In winter, let nature take its course, but water a little if you have several weeks without rain.

• **POTTING**
In the spring, every 2 to 3 years in a well-drained pot with soil for acid-loving plants.

Rooting cuttings in soil / method 1

1. Cut stems 4 to 6 inches long (10 to 15 cm); they must be healthy and recent (of the year) but already rigid. Make sure they don't show any signs of disease or pests. Remove all the leaves; do not keep any.

2. Prepare a pot about 4 inches (10 cm) in diameter, fill with seedling soil, make a hole in it, and plant your stem upside down! This avoids the risk of rot.

3. The cut end that remains in the open will heal in two to three weeks. You can then turn the cutting in the right direction, burying the stem two-thirds of its length. Place a bell jar or a plastic bottle atop the pot to create a greenhouse effect. Place the pot in a bright, warm place above 40°F (5°C).

4. You will then have to wait all winter, watching that the soil remains moist. Water as soon as it dries on the surface.

5. From the following spring, in March or April, you can repot your cutting in a larger pot filled with soil for roses!

▶ ▶ ▶

Rooting cuttings in soil / method 2

1 Cut stems of 4 to 6 inches (10 to 15 cm), they must be healthy and recent (from that year), but already rigid. Make sure they don't show any signs of disease or pests.

2 Cut the stems just under a node and keep five to six leaves at its end. Cut off the tips of the stems and cut the leaves in half.

3 Prepare a pot filled with liquid fungicide and soak your cuttings in it for a few minutes.

4 Plant them in a pot filled with seedling soil. Place a glass or plastic cloche over the pot to create a greenhouse effect. Place the jar in a bright, heated place between 65°F–75°F (18°C–24°C).

5 You will then have to wait all winter, watching that the soil remains moist. Water as soon as it dries on the surface.

6 From the following spring, in March or April, you can repot your cutting in a larger pot filled with soil suitable for roses!

Polka dot begonia

Begonia maculata

ALL THOSE WHO LOVE ORIGINAL FOLIAGES WILL TAKE PLEASURE IN GROWING THE POLKA DOT BEGONIA! IT OFFERS SUMPTUOUS GREEN FOLIAGE SPLASHED WITH WHITE AND SILVER.

Family: Begoniaceae
Origin: Brazil
Best time to take a cutting: winter, in the rest period after flowering
TAKES ROOT IN WATER OR SOIL, FROM A STEM

Plant care

- **EXPOSURE**
Bright, out of direct sunlight and away from heat sources.
- **WATERING / MAINTENANCE**
– In winter, water as soon as the soil dries on the surface, once a week.
– In spring and summer, 2 to 3 times a week.
Remove faded flowers as you go, this stimulates new flowering.
- **NUTRIENTS**
From April to the end of September, bring it liquid fertilizer for flowering plants.
- **POTTING**
Every three years, in the spring.

Rooting cuttings in water

1. Take a stem 2 or 3 inches (5 to 8 cm) long. Remove the leaves to leave only three or four at the end. Immerse the stem in the water, making sure to keep its head above water.

2. As soon as the first roots are an inch long (3 cm), it's time to put it in a pot.

3. Use a pot about 4 inches (10 cm) in diameter. Fill it with seedling soil: a light, fine and draining soil. This type of soil is ideal for promoting the rooting of the cutting. Make a hole in the soil to gently slip the cutting into it, without damaging the roots, then cover them by packing lightly.

4. Place the pot in a bright place, without direct sun and warm 68°F–75°F (20°C–24°C) and water as soon as the soil dries on the surface.

5. Water regularly to keep the soil moist and watch for signs of development: new leaves and elongation of the stem.

Rooting cuttings in soil

1. Take a stem that has at least three nodes. Remove the leaves to leave only three or four at the end.

2. In a pot filled with seedling soil, make a hole, and plant the cutting there. Pack the soil well around the stem. Water well to moisten the soil.

3. Place the pot in a bright and warm place 68°F–75°F (20°C–24°C) and water as soon as the soil dries on the surface.

4. When new leaves develop, you can then repot the plant in a slightly larger pot with a good quality potting soil.

Aloe barbadensis

Aloe vera

ESSENTIAL ALOE VERA, WELL KNOWN FOR ITS SOOTHING PROPERTIES, IS VERY GENEROUS WITH ITS "MEDICINE".

Family: Aloeaceae
Origin: Mediterranean region, North Africa, Canary Islands, and Cape Verde
Best time to take a cutting: spring
TAKES ROOT IN THE GROUND, FROM A SUCKER OR A LEAF

Plant care

- **EXPOSURE**
Sunny.
- **WATERING**
– In winter, water when the soil is completely dry (about once a month).
– In spring and summer, water when the top 1 to 1½ inches (3 to 4 cm) of soil is dry (about every 15 days).
- **NUTRIENTS**
Give it liquid fertilizer for every two weeks during periods of growth.
- **POTTING**
In spring, every 2 or 3 years.

Propagation by offset

1. Unpot the plant to be divided and carefully remove the soil surrounding the offset by hand. Then take the "volunteer" by keeping a maximum of roots which will increase its chances of recovery.

2. Place it in a pot filled with light potting soil (composed of soil and peat), burying it lightly, its heart should not be underground. Don't water right away.

3. Place the pot in the light (without direct sunlight), in a room at a minimum temperature of 65°F (18°C), kept away from drafts.

4. After fifteen days, water lightly and let dry completely before watering again.

Leaf cutting

1. This technique does not take easily, but it can be tried! Cut a leaf of about 3 or 4 inches (8 to 10 cm), among the oldest, located at the base of the plant. Preferably use a knife; pruning shears would crush the fleshy leaf too much and damage it. Allow the leaf to air dry for two to three days. This is the time it takes for a healing callus to form at the cut end.

2. Place about a third of the leaf in the ground, straight, in a pot with holes, using a mixture of well-draining compost lightened with sand, in equal proportion, with clay pellets at the bottom of the pot.

3. Then mist the soil to slightly moisten the surface.

4 Place your cutting away from drafts and direct sunlight and mist once a week to moisten the soil.

5 Wait several weeks. To check if the cutting has taken: in the best case, you will have the pleasure of watching the growth of a new leaf. Otherwise, pull the twig lightly. If there is resistance, it is a sign that the roots have developed and taken well!

Chain of hearts

Ceropegia woodii

THIS WAXY PLANT WITH ITS PRETTY, HEART-SHAPED FOLIAGE IS IRRESISTIBLE! EASY TO MAINTAIN, IT FITS IN ANY ROOM IN THE HOUSE AND WILL OFFER YOU BEAUTIFUL PINK FLOWERS.

Family: Asclepiadaceae
Origin: South Africa
Best time to take a cutting: year-round
TAKES ROOT IN SOIL FROM A STEM, OR BY LAYERING

Plant care

- **EXPOSURE**
Bright, sunny during the cooler hours of the day.
- **WATERING**
– In spring and summer, every ten days. give it fertilizer for succulents, Once a month over the same period.
– From the arrival of autumn and until the end of winter, 1 to 2 waterings per month are sufficient.
– Do not let the water stagnate in the saucer.
- **POTTING**
In the spring, every two years.

Rooting cuttings in soil

1 Cut a stem at least 2 inches (5 cm) long, keeping a tuber (that is to say the small, white ball that serves as a water reserve and that will have formed on the foliage). Leave to dry for a day to ensure proper healing.

2 In a pot filled with seedling soil, bury half of the tuber and a small portion of the stem.

3 Place your cutting in a bright place without direct sunlight and in a heated room between 60°F and 68°F (15°C and 20°C). Water regularly to keep the soil moist.

4 You will then have to wait several weeks before seeing the rooting of your cutting! The waiting time can vary: in spring or summer, about three weeks, in winter, about six weeks.

Layering

This technique is ideal if you want to flesh out your plant.

1 Prepare a pot with drainage holes, place clay pellets in the bottom, then fill with seedling soil.

2 On a mother plant, select a stem (without cutting it) that has a knot at the level of a double leaf, bend it without breaking it, so as to push the knot into the soil of your pot. Then fix the stem to the ground, using small pins to prevent it from moving.

3 Water to keep the soil moist until the node forms a tuber, after three to six weeks depending on the season. You can then separate the cutting from the plant by cutting the stem that connects them.

Echeveria

Echeveria

SAME TECHNIQUE
Jade plant

THESE INTRICATE LITTLE PLANTS, VERY SIMPLE TO MAINTAIN, ARE ALWAYS APPRECIATED AND IDEAL FOR THOSE WHO DO NOT YET HAVE A GREEN THUMB OR ARE OFTEN AWAY FROM HOME. WITH THEIR VARIED FOLIAGES IN PASTEL COLORS, THEY ARE VERY DECORATIVE.

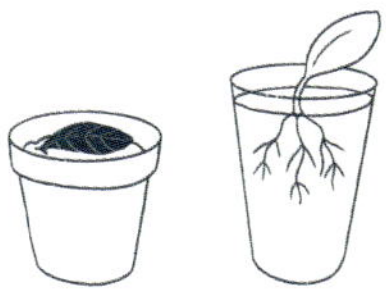

Family: Crassulaceae
Origin: Mexico
Best time to take a cutting: year-round, excluding freezing temperatures
Takes root in soil or water, from a leaf

Plant care

- **EXPOSURE**
Bright, indirect light.
- **WATERING**
– In winter, soak it once a month.
– In spring and autumn, once every 15 days.
– In summer, once a week. Let it soak for about thirty minutes.
Wait until the soil dries between waterings.
Remove faded leaves as you go, as this stimulates development.
- **POTTING**
Annually, in a slightly larger pot in the spring. Use succulent soil or potting mix and sand.

Leaf cutting in soil

1 Take three healthy leaves (to increase your chances of success) by detaching them with a dry gesture from the base of the plant. Let them dry for three to four days until a callus appears.

2 Put some soil for succulents in a pot and lay the leaves on it without pushing them down. Place your cuttings in an airy and bright room.

3 Mist the soil every day and arm yourself with patience until the arrival of small roots, it can take up to four weeks.

4 Mini rosettes (new leaves) will then develop. It will then be necessary to water less often, about once every two weeks.

5 When a mini rosette is well formed, you can gently dig it up by hand to transplant it into a separate pot, just for it!

TIPS
Always cut several leaves to increase your chances of success, as not all of them will take.

Leaf cuttings in water

1 Take three healthy leaves by detaching them from the base of the plant. Let them dry for three to four days until a callus appears.

2 In a transparent vase with a narrow neck, add your cuttings so that the callus is bathed in water.

3 After two to three weeks, the first roots should appear. When they reach a half an inch (1 cm) in length, it is time to place them in a pot filled with potting soil for succulents. Bury the roots very lightly. You must then follow the steps mentioned opposite for the cutting in the ground.

Haworthia fascinata

Haworthia

NARROW AND POINTED, WITH DARK GREEN FOLIAGE SPOTTED WITH WHITE SPOTS, THE HAWORTHIA PRODUCES LOTS OF "BABIES"!

Family: Xanthorrhoeaceae
Origin: South Africa
Best time to take a cutting: year-round, indoors only in winter
TAKES ROOT IN SOIL FROM A SHOOT, OR IN WATER FROM A LEAF

Plant care

- **EXPOSURE**
Bright, indirect light.
- **WATERING**
– In winter, soak it once a month.
– In spring and autumn, bathe it once every 15 days, and in summer, once a week.
Let it soak for about thirty minutes. Wait until the soil dries between waterings. Remove faded leaves as you go, which stimulates its development.
- **POTTING**
Every two years in spring, in soil for succulents. Place clay pellets at the bottom of the pot to aid drainage. Do not leave water in the saucer.

Rooting an offset in soil

1. Unpot the plant to be divided and carefully remove the soil surrounding the offset by hand. Collect it while keeping as many roots as possible, which will increase its chances of recovery.

2. Place it in a pot filled with light potting soil, made up of soil and peat, burying it lightly, the bulk of the plant should be above ground. Don't water right away.

3. Place the pot in the light (without direct sunlight), in a room with a minimum temperature of 65°F (18°C), kept away from drafts.

4. After fifteen days, water lightly and let dry completely before watering again.

Rooting an offset in water

1. As for the soil technique, choose an offset to clear, taking care to keep as many roots as possible. Let it dry for two to three days to dry out any scars.

2. Place your young shoot in water at room temperature, making sure to immerse the roots well and keep the leaves out of the water. Place it away from drafts and direct sunlight, which could damage both its leaves and the roots that develop, then wait.

3. After a few days...surprise! Small white roots form. It is then time to plant your cutting in the ground (see page 23).

Cut the leaves into 3-inch (8cm) sections.

Plant the cut part in the ground at an angle.

Cover with a jar to create a greenhouse effect.

Wait a few months and you'll have a plant like this!

Snake plant

Sansevieria

THIS BULLET-PROOF PLANT IS A GREAT CHOICE FOR BEGINNERS. IT'S EASY TO MAINTAIN, AND REQUIRES VERY LITTLE ATTENTION.

Family: Asparagaceae
Origi: Africa
Best time to take a cutting: spring and summer, the heat ensures a better grip of the cuttings.
TAKES ROOT IN SOIL, FROM A LEAF

Plant care

- **EXPOSURE**

Bright, without direct sun which could yellow its foliage, 65°F to 72°F (18°C–22°C). A lack of light slows its growth.

- **WATERING**

– In spring and summer, once a week.
– In winter, once every three weeks or so.

- **POTTING**

Re-pot every two years using cactus soil and a slightly larger terracotta pot.

Rooting leaves in soil

1. Take a leaf. Cut sections of about 3 inches (8 cm), using a clean knife. Cut the base of each section diagonally on each side so that the part, which you will put in the ground, is narrower. Allow three days to dry for wounds to heal.

2. Prepare, for each section, a well-drained hole 4 inches (10 cm) in diameter, with clay pellets at the bottom that you can water immediately.

3. Then plant the sections, taking care to plant the cut side at an angle. Place a glass or plastic cover on the jar, which will need to be removed for about ten minutes each day to avoid condensation.

4. After four weeks, roots will begin to grow at the base of the stump. Then it's time to remove the bell.

Index of plants cited

Index of techniques

Books that inspire us

- Denis Retournard, Rosenn Le Page, *L'ABC de la bouture*, Rustica, 1999
- Fran Bailey, Zia Allaway, *Le Petit Larousse des plantes d'intérieur*, Larousse, 2019
- Andrew Mikolajski, *100 fiches spéciales boutures*, Marabout, 2019
- Caro Langton, Rose Ray, *Les plantes & la maison*, Trad. Sylvie Lagorce, Rouergue, 2017

We are four friends—Charles, Tiphaine, François and Olivia—on a Maison Bouture adventure, which began in 2017. Amazed by nature and what it offers, we were sure that it would be a resource for others, and we wanted to give teaching a central place in our lives.

It is important to us to share our experience with you so that you can cut your plants endlessly; we want them to be healthy and flourish!

Charles, our landscaper, is the one who has the best knowledge of plants and shares his knowledge with us. His advice is invaluable!

Tiphaine is responsible for the image of Maison Bouture. She photographs nature and takes care to highlight it. Every day, she also takes the time to answer your messages and to accompany you and advise you in the best way possible in the maintenance and cuttings of your plants.

François, eager for novelties and challenges, makes every effort to ensure that our Ephemeral Gardens unfold and shine throughout France, as close as possible to you.

Olivia carefully processes and prepares each of your online orders. She is constantly looking to find you new plants, beautiful and rare, and new models of pots and planters to enhance your plants. She also provides customer service.

Gingko Press
English language edition first published in March 2023

ISBN: 978-1-58423-777-8

Translated and adapted by: David Lopes
Typesetting: Amy Jasinski
Copyediting: Bridget Manzella
Proofreading: Katie Edwards

Originally published in the French Language as Noyaux & Boutures

Direction: Jean-Louis Hocq
Direction éditoriale: Corinne Cesano
Édition: Iris Odier et Françoise Caille
Collaboration éditoriale: Anaïs Guichard
Correction: Pascale Braud
Conception graphique: Manon Bucciarelli
Mise en page: Istria
Photographies: Tiphaine Germain-Lacour
Illustrations: Léa Morineau
Fabrication: Céline Premel-Cabic et Camille Friquet

FSC www.fsc.org MIX Paper from responsible sources FSC® C106600